KINGDOM PIONEERS

Copyright © 2024 by Rhea Falig

Published by Arrows & Stones

All rights reserved. No portion of this book may be reproduced, stored in a retrieval system, or transmitted in any form or by any means—electronic, mechanical, photocopy, recording, scanning, or other—except for brief quotations in critical reviews or articles, without prior written permission of the author.

Scripture quotations marked AMP are taken from the Amplified® Bible, Copyright © 2015 by The Lockman Foundation. Used by permission. lockman.org. | Scripture quotations marked ESV are from The ESV® Bible (The Holy Bible, English Standard Version®), copyright © 2001 by Crossway, a publishing ministry of Good News Publishers. Used by permission. All rights reserved. | Scripture quotations marked KJV are taken from the King James Version of the Bible. Public domain. | Scripture quotations marked MSG are taken from THE MESSAGE, copyright © 1993, 1994, 1995, 1996, 2000, 2001, 2002 by Eugene H. Peterson. Used by permission of NavPress. All rights reserved. Represented by Tyndale House Publishers, Inc. | Scripture quotations marked NIV are taken from the Holy Bible, New International Version®, NIV®. Copyright © 1973, 1978, 1984, 2011 by Biblica, Inc.™ Used by permission of Zondervan. All rights reserved worldwide. www.zondervan.com. The "NIV" and "New International Version" are trademarks registered in the United States Patent and Trademark Office by Biblica, Inc.™ | Scripture quotations marked NLT are taken from the Holy Bible, New Living Translation, copyright © 1996, 2004, 2015 by Tyndale House Foundation. Used by permission of Tyndale House Publishers, Inc., Carol Stream, Illinois 60188. All rights reserved. | Scripture quotations marked TPT are from The Passion Translation®. Copyright © 2017, 2018 by Passion & Fire Ministries, Inc. Used by permission. All rights reserved. ThePassionTranslation.com. |

For foreign and subsidiary rights, contact the author.

Cover design by Sara Young
Cover photo by Josiah Falig

ISBN: 978-1-962401-28-9   1 2 3 4 5 6 7 8 9 10

Printed in the United States of America

PURIFIED. POSITIONED. PRIESTHOOD.

THE CALL FOR A PURIFIED,
POSITIONED, PRIESTHOOD TO
RETURN TO THE FATHERS HEART
AND PIONEER WILD RIVERS OF
PERSONAL REVIVAL

Contents

Acknowledgements vii

CHAPTER 1. The River 9

CHAPTER 2. The Oil Lamp 51

CHAPTER 3. The Broken Ladder 97

CHAPTER 4. The Résumé 123

CHAPTER 5. The Woodchipper 153

CHAPTER 6. The Priesthood 215

CHAPTER 7. The Pioneer 267

Acknowledgements

To my husband, Eric, who has contended by my side for decades of ministry with a mutual longing to see family altars restored, Levites discipled, priests purified, and the days of idolizing positions and platforms over and done. Traveling with you by my side has made the narrow way much less lonely. Thanks for risking it all to lead our family to high and holy ground. Thanks for championing my calling. As gifted as you are, your talent and anointing are the least interesting things about you, and that's saying a lot. Your song is mighty, but the true groundswell of worship is your private life.

The real gold to me will always be how you've selflessly loved and served your family in private. How your hands have stayed glued to this plow, even when you were pushing it through valleys of the shadow of death. Inner court ministry to Jesus and the ministry flowing inside our home have remained your most sacred calling. The most profound work of your life will not be something you've done or how others have perceived you from afar—but the oil you stored, the tables you built, the altar you stayed on, the flesh you killed, the sons you fathered, and the wife you loved like Jesus. I suspect we will enjoy the fruit of your integrity and intentionality for generations to come. I love you.

To my sons Josiah, David, and Judah. My sweetest encouragers. Constant reminders of the kindness of God. This book was written as a road map for you. There is legacy, treasure, and oil to be discovered in these pages. I pray that it will prepare you for the challenges you may face as you pick up your mantle and live lives of yieldedness to the Father that is anything but ordinary. That the battles I've fought—you will never have to. The purity of your love for Jesus and the weightiness of the anointing resting on your lives will take you places beyond your capacity to even dream, think, or imagine. And your Christlike character will keep you there for the long haul.

Being your mother is like being the foundation of a great cathedral. I've always known you would be my most important calling and my absolute favorite adventure. May your identity be firmly rooted in the voice of your heavenly Father, and may you never spend a second yoked to the rejection or fear of man. You are fully loved, and you have nothing to earn. Stay wild. Jesus is the prize.

To my mother, Tisa. Everything I know about grit, perseverance, and unapologetic authenticity, I have learned from you. I adore you. Thank you for your constant support and unwavering love.

To Jesus—May You receive Your full reward.

CHAPTER 1
The River

At the end of 2019, during a very confusing and painful season of transition and grief, I wrote down this simple word I felt the Lord drop in my spirit one day: *I'm calling you to write a book for the church that will be a road map back to My heart.* I feel it would do a huge disservice if I were to lie to you in these pages, so I'm committed to staying appropriately vulnerable throughout our entire journey together. To be honest, when God spoke that word, I initially thought He meant He was going to download new, creative church-growth recipes and marketing strategies that would help train and equip churches to be the gold standard of excellence in their communities, attract consumers, and help their brand run like a well-oiled corporate machine with lots of spiritual sounding undertones.

Basically, it would have been a book about how to climb a ladder and control a river. It probably would have been well-received in some circles, but clearly, that was *not* the book God wanted from me, and clearly, *I* needed freedom from the performance-driven ministry mindsets that had been poured into my foundation. I needed to return to the very basics of

His heart for the church. Before I could do that, I needed to return to the very basics of His heart for *me*. This isn't a book of condemnation, pointing out all the ways we're faulty. This book invites us to empty ourselves of the things that are killing us anyway, so we can be filled to overflowing with the fullness of His river. So if any of the content steps on your toes, please find comfort in knowing it stepped on mine *first*, and I'm still finding pieces of toe just lying around in random places.

For as long as I can remember, I knew God had called me to be a scribe of His heart. I've been faithfully collecting and stewarding those words for decades with my ear pressed against His chest. I knew there were messages for the church inside me waiting to be released. Over and over, the Lord would confirm it through the Holy Spirit, His Word, and the people of God. How and when and where were questions too big for me to answer and entirely up to *His* timing. It was always, *One day I'll . . .* (fill in the blank). What if the emptying, breaking, and purifying you've walked through are really preparation and pruning because your "one day" is closer than you think it is?

THE WORK HE WANTS TO DO THROUGH YOU, HE WILL ALWAYS BEGIN IN YOU.

I've never wanted to be a self-made person. I know the dangers of moving ahead of God. I couldn't control His timing any more than I could turn the tide or control how the river rolls. What I didn't anticipate was how fast and wild and powerfully that river would carry me off on my *own* pioneering journey toward freedom and reformation. Then we had a global pandemic which gave me lots and lots of time in the river. By the time it was over, there was no desire left in me to ever go back to normal. The work He wants to do through you, He will always begin IN you. I'm guessing if you're reading this book, it's because you're looking for answers to the unsettled feeling constantly lingering in the back of your mind telling you, *This can't be all there is. There has to be more.* If that's you, you don't have to chase revival, my friend. Revival is chasing *you*. And it has been for a while. Jesus is revival. Simply step into the river, and see where it leads you.

After the word about the book, I had a dream. In the dream, the Holy Spirit was breathing over rivers, and His breath was pushing ships forward tasked with carrying this specific message to the church about returning to His heart. No two ships looked identical, but they were all carrying the same message to the north, south, east, and west. Sails were being repaired and readied to catch the wind of the Father's heart to announce to His bride, "It's time to return to the river." Time to remove the mixture and return to the purity of what it means to be beloved. It's time to stop striving for the very things Christ emptied Himself of: status, equality with God, reputation, position, entitlement, and the esteem of men. No amount of outward excellence and adornment can mask our true inner condition.

Our value has grown far too attached to systems built by man that, one day, will turn to dust. One day, many will lay down the systems they built as an offering to the Lord. They'll say, "Look what we did in Your name. Look what we built for your glory." And He'll respond, "Depart from Me, I never knew you." I don't know how you imagine the tone of His voice will be while He's saying that. But for me, His voice is cracking, and His heart is breaking. I don't think they're going to be easy words for Him to say. Because it was never about the systems; it was always about staying in the river and doing the will of the Father.

What if your church doesn't need another program, conference, or social media campaign? What if it's not about adding more but removing excess? What if we're all so tired and prone to quit because we've built entire belief systems on how to control an uncontrollable river? What if simply inviting Jesus into the room really is *enough*? After the journey I've been on, I'm convinced it is. I have experiential evidence that it is.

WHAT IF IT'S NOT ABOUT ADDING MORE BUT REMOVING EXCESS?

We've seen neighbors come to Jesus in our living room, and we didn't have to give them a discount code to our coffee shop to get them there. Our teenagers don't rush to leave the room if the preaching is "boring." They don't get annoyed if the worship is too long because we've discipled them to know that the church doesn't exist for their entertainment. They stay and engage in prayer and conversation with seventy-year-olds about life and Scripture because the young people inside our churches actually don't want another pizza party for bringing a friend to church. They're smarter and more capable than we give them credit for, and they are starving for *substance* and for people to be real with them. (And yes, pizza, too, because ... they are teenagers!)

You see, this river isn't for one generation. It's for *all* generations gathered around the only thing that's really needed—Jesus. There is a revival sweeping across the earth. The remnant returning to the power and simplicity of Acts and prodigals coming home. Gathering, sending, caring, healing, sharing, miracles, meals, deliverance, discipleship, bread, new wine, and a purified, positioned, priesthood of *all* believers.

Hospitality is one thing; manipulation is another. If you want entitlement and consumerism removed from your church, you have to start looking more closely at the systems that are rewarding it. We give out gold stars just for showing up and breathing. We feel undervalued and underappreciated if the pastor doesn't give us a shout-out for doing the bare minimum we signed up to do. We ask God to use us and then feel used when He does. Entitlement is making the church weak, and it's conditioning people to think they can't live without it. It's causing a generation to amalgamate its identity with assignments and titles. What's even more concerning is that preferences have replaced Christlikeness as the standard by which we measure if something is healthy or not.

When you're done looking at the systems that could be perpetuating entitlement, ask the Lord to take you even deeper into the insecurities and places that lacked identity and established those systems in the first place. If we want to stay in the river, we have to die to the fear of never measuring up. The fear of man keeps us yoked to the approval of people. If we've got the river of God living in our bellies, but we're still seeking the approval and honor of people, that's where it will stay indefinitely. And the fruitfulness of our ministries and legacy will be just as dried up as that river. That will *not* be your story.

John 5:41-42 (author paraphrase) says, "I do not accept the honor that comes from men, for I know what kind of people you really are, and I can see that the love of God has found no home in you." Therefore, this book wasn't written with an agenda to profit or make a name for myself. As far as I'm concerned, God can burn up all my platforms from now until the end of time because I'm learning to live dead to the approval of man. But I do believe wholeheartedly that the pleasure of the Father rests on the message of this book and that it carries an anointing to set captives free and realign the pioneers who have gotten off course back to the One Thing that matters. Not *because* of me but in spite of me. I believe you're reading it because God is inviting you into a holy reset of priorities, ambitions, and mindsets.

I BELIEVE YOU'RE READING IT BECAUSE GOD IS INVITING YOU INTO A HOLY RESET OF PRIORITIES, AMBITIONS, AND MINDSETS.

I have bathed this project in His presence and laid it as an offering at His feet. I've asked Him to purify and refine every word on every page so that you could receive it exactly how the Father wants you to. Anything that may fall short of that objective is a reflection of me—not Him. Many months have been spent in prayer and fasting. I have leaned into His voice, studied Scripture, rested under the covering of healthy community, and received counsel from voices much wiser than my own. This book was not born out of human effort or striving but complete abiding. As I would soak in His presence, the river of His love would begin to flow into the pages of this book. Even now, it's my prayer that you will feel the oppression of old seasons blow away like ash in the wind and a fresh gust of hope will fill your sails. That you will be drenched by waves of love. Wrecked and undone by His goodness.

While I only spent a week (quite literally morning, noon, and night) writing this book like there was a holy fire shut up inside my bones, it has actually been fleshed out in my own walk for decades. I'm not some clout chaser who just wants a book deal and a platform. I'm coming from over twenty years of ministry experience. I've won some battles and gained some authority and insight to speak into these things. I've also made more than my share of costly mistakes along the way and have learned very painful lessons. I'm so grateful that He redeems the failures of our past. I'm so glad that how we mishandled one season doesn't disqualify us from being trusted to try again in another. Every day, I drink from a fountain called mercy.

I've been rejected, deceived, misunderstood, set up, attacked, mocked, betrayed, silenced, accused, abused, and used but *never* by God. Sometimes, His kids behave badly and misrepresent Him, but the same flowing river that removes you from toxic people will carry you forward to family. Your enemies come at you from one direction, but they're scattering from you in seven. The problem is giving up on God and the church because of past trauma. We're out of danger, but we're also out of the healthy connection and community that God established for our health, growth, and protection. We can't say we love God and hate the things that God loves.

Leaving our assignment, calling, and community aren't the only ways the church self-protects. We're also good at covering our wounds with a false sense of significance, projects and events, and titles and positions. We busy ourselves so people can't see how broken we are. The rest and healing you need are only found in letting Christ embrace you as a son or daughter. Come back to the river.

The house that broke you probably won't be the house that heals you. But God *does* have healthy, safe people waiting for you, and He will increase your discernment to recognize them. You won't always have to run to isolation in self-protect mode or be hypervigilant about everything that could be wrong. That will no longer be your default button. A day is coming when you'll be able to open your heart up and trust again. Believe for it.

Your trauma is not too complicated for the Healer. You're not a problem to solve. You're not too much to handle. You're not the black sheep you were made to feel like. The enemy is such a liar. Some of you have an inner dialogue that plays like a broken record in your head, *This cycle is never gonna end. I'm always gonna be stuck. I'm always gonna be rejected and broken. Nobody will ever understand me. I'm always gonna be a vagabond doomed to a life of isolation. People will always walk away. I'm never gonna find where I belong.*

No matter how well the enemy can preach a lie, that's *not* your legacy. His words only hold power if we come into agreement with them. In fact, you should go ahead and just believe the exact opposite of anything he says. I've been around the block and have seen it *all*, yet my love for the church has only deepened *through* it all. Because I stayed in the river, and the river stayed in me.

That is my legacy. That is yours too.

Any deconstruction of my paper boat has been reconstructed into something solid and seaworthy by the hands of a loving Captain. I'm not speaking from a place of unresolved conflict or bitterness. I'm speaking from the overflow of a heart that's been wildly healed and transformed. If He's whispering to your heart, this book is an invitation to respond. Not because my words are wise and magical but because His heart for you is resting on them. He has so much more for you. You are what I call a *Kingdom Pioneer*. There are paths you haven't seen, and places He still wants to take you in His heart. Your best days are still ahead of you.

The Father is set on seeing His sons and daughters free, so they can pioneer the dreams He's planted inside of them. He wants you to travel light and unencumbered by the painful yokes of past seasons. He's removing the tattered, battle-weary, worn-out garments and replacing them with clean, fresh priestly ones. You're returning to your First Love. Jesus warned the church that in the last days, our love would wax cold. The road would be so hard and long that we'd stop loving the way He's called us to. The love you lost in the last season is returning. Including your love for people. He wants to excavate the places you've been ministering out of pain instead of healing and fear instead of love, so His redemption can be released through your message instead of poisoned darts of offense.

It's time for the church to step into a holy realignment with the flow of His river. God wants to heal wounded worshipers. He wants to heal the leader with poison arrows hanging out of their back while they continue to tend to sheep at altars, unaware that they still are one. We never graduate from the floor. We never reach a place of maturity where we'll stop needing the Good Shepherd to pull us in close and tend to our wounds.

He wants to deliver saints from entitlement and elitism and consumerism. He wants the backbiting, devouring, and dishonoring of our spiritual siblings to stop. All of that is rooted in an orphan spirit because we don't understand sonship. He wants healthy teams that help people heal, not add to their pain and trauma. He wants our agendas and motivations purified. He wants to gently correct Levites who have turned holy ground into platforms to prop up egos and the pastors who have enabled performance over presence and talent over anointing for far too long.

Things are in forward motion. This river is leading us to a wedding. He's purifying the bride and making wrong things right and bringing darkness into the light of His love not to shame and expose but to heal and restore. He is calling us back into pure kingdom alignment. The right model for this reformation isn't copying the wineskin next door or the social media influencer with the blue check by their name. It's quick obedience to your own unique assignment. And here's the beautiful part! People don't have to understand you, follow you, or even agree with you. It doesn't matter what was said or done against you. Your obedience is only contingent upon one thing—YOU. What Christ has done *in* you will always be greater than what man can do *to* you.

> **WHAT CHRIST HAS DONE IN YOU WILL ALWAYS BE GREATER THAN WHAT MAN CAN DO TO YOU.**

His river leads to deep places of rest. Rest is holy. Rest is productive. Rest is a rhythm of His heart. He commanded it and modeled it. It will help you keep the main things first. Rest will save your marriage. It will realign you with God's design for family. It will sustain your ministry and reset your values. It will exponentially increase your effectiveness. Rest will help you see the value of people instead of looking at them as commodities to enhance your image. I'm not talking about a nice Sunday nap kind of rest. That is an essential aspect of it, but when the Bible commands us to rest, it is inviting us into deeper connection with God. To lay down the striving. To trust Him.

I traded programs and formulas for the purity of a wild unshakable kingdom with untamed King Jesus at the helm. In His river, there is nothing left to earn or prove. Nobody to impress. There is work to do and order in His government, but it's all flowing from joyful delight—not religious, pharisaical duty. Just you and Him. Leaning into new rhythms. Learning to serve from rest instead of striving. So much more gets accomplished when we stop resisting the flow of His river. God values rest. All striving submits to God's gift of Sabbath rest.

I also believe Scripture teaches us that God places value on names. God would often reassign new names to speak of new identities. One day, we're all going to receive a new name on a white stone. The name Rhea means "Flowing River." I grew up surrounded by wild Missouri rivers. We'd spend summers camping with friends. Fishing on the river was our reward for a hard day of farming. I would often look out and see eagles flying above the cliffs of the James River from the perch of my bedroom window. I never wasted a perfectly good opportunity to be the first to jump in a river and emerge soaking wet—clothes and all.

I believe the physical often parallels what's happening in the spiritual. My name and childhood desire to be near the river by my home reflects the present reality that I was meant to live in the flowing river of God and invite others to this river as well. I wonder what's in your name and what hidden gems the Lord has buried under your own wild rivers waiting to be pulled out and discovered. The only way to find out is to get off the shore and step into the river for yourself. Some things can only be found when you move beyond the safety of the shore. One thing is for sure: what you've walked through wasn't for nothing. Jesus transforms pain into someone else's road map to healing. It's a promise from God that the comfort you received from Him will be the same comfort others receive *through* you. John 7:37-38 (TPT) says, "All you thirsty ones, come to me! Come to me and drink! Believe in me so that rivers of living water will burst out from within you, flowing from your innermost being, just like the Scripture says!" Be comforted and comfort others.

The truth I share in this book preceded much personal breaking. The oil of this offering to the Lord isn't careless or cheap. Like King David, I don't want to give God an offering that cost me nothing. It is the fragrance of my broken-up heart on His altar and a lifetime journey toward deep inner healing and deliverance from performance-driven ministry mindsets.

I had spent years learning all the leadership principles a three-pound brain can carry. My notes are more like manuscripts. I have boxes and boxes full of church growth recipes. I honor those lessons and the people who shared them, so please don't misunderstand my heart here. But being a student of the Holy Spirit requires unlearning formulas and stepping into the river for yourself. It can't be manufactured or studied in a classroom.

If we don't repair the holes in our sails, we'll spend a lifetime going in circles and calling it progress, like the Israelites taking forty years to make an eleven-day journey. God has more for you and me. It's a glory to glory story. We always want to honor and celebrate what God has done, but our best adventures are *ahead* of us. There are realms of His glory we haven't even begun to touch. As my grandpa would say, "We've only wet our whistle." There are unmapped rivers of the Father's heart He is inviting you to explore and pioneer a path for others to follow.

THERE ARE UNMAPPED RIVERS OF THE FATHER'S HEART HE IS INVITING YOU TO EXPLORE AND PIONEER A PATH FOR OTHERS TO FOLLOW.

He is crying out for a people who will repair the sails and catch the wind of His Spirit. We need strong sails and a sturdy ship to get to where we're going because it isn't smooth sailing. The waters get choppy when we say yes to new horizons and wineskins. The storms you'll face have shipwrecked even the most experienced voyagers. We need the fresh wind of the Spirit blowing us into uncharted waters, and we need the steadfast rudder of Scripture keeping us anchored and aligned with our Captain. One thing is certain. We cannot stay where we've been. Our inheritance lies beyond familiar streams.

In my own journey, God stripped down my ivory tower to its very foundation until I looked up to the heavens and cried, "What is left to build on?" But what felt like death was actually the doorway to true living. I'll tell you what the Lord whispered to me in case you find yourself in a similar boat: *There is a lot left to build on. And it's time you allow Me to remove the wallpaper you've used to patch the holes in the walls and tear down the decorations you've used to disguise the decay and let me build something truly lasting and beautiful in you.*

We can rest assured:

> The Lord will guide you continually, giving you water when you are dry and restoring your strength. You

will be like a well-watered garden, like an ever-flowing spring. Some of you will rebuild the deserted ruins of your cities. Then you will be known as a rebuilder of walls and a restorer of homes. —Isaiah 58:11-12 (NLT)

You cannot rebuild ancient ruins, repair the breach, and restore homes when your own frame is collapsing around you. I can't think of a greater tragedy than using your gifts to see other walls restored while your own walls crumble. Seeing other families restored while your own family lies in ruins. You can't give others a drink from a dried-up riverbed. What do flight attendants always say? Put your own oxygen mask on *first*. We're good to nobody if we're spiritually dead. Yet so many of us are on life support, building with broken hammers, and the Lord is inviting us into a place of real living and wholeness so we can be contributors instead of liabilities on the mission fields we're called to. Your most important ministry will always be first to the Lord and next in your home.

Am I saying our lives have to be perfect before God can use us? That we somehow have to earn a ticket into the river? Get cleaned up first? Do something worthy enough to be noticed and qualified? Absolutely not. The blood of Jesus is sufficient. The Lord is so kind and gracious that He can use our gifts even when our hearts are far from Him, and we're living in hidden bondage and sin. He can use a donkey too, but if being a donkey is the goal of our lives, we may want to set the bar higher.

The Lord is warning us to tend to the condition of our own house. We received an invitation to restore the family altar in 2020. The Lord shut down everything, so parents could pastor their own kids again, couples could repair the breach in their marriage, eternity could be practiced around dinner tables, and revival fires could be tended in our homes. For some, there was no going back to normal, but for others, I feel it grieved the Father to see His children choosing to go back to a normal that was killing them and rejecting the rescue of His hand because the river was uncomfortable and unfamiliar. New wineskins often are. Like the rich young ruler, everything we truly desire and need is found in Jesus, but the cost of giving up our precious programs is more than we're willing to pay. So we trade eternal rewards for temporary tithes, attendees, and attaboys.

Forming ungodly mindsets is easy. The enemy lies. We unknowingly partner with him. The longer his lies stay, the deeper they take root. Recognizing them is the tricky part, especially when some of those lies have become values we celebrate in church culture. (Like performance-driven ministry.) But there is no lie God's love cannot dismantle. The hardest part of this dismantling was not letting go of my dreams. The hardest part was realizing how deeply my value was still yoked to them instead of to Jesus.

The heart of this book isn't to hype you up on change for the sake of change. Who even has space for that? Not me! Ask my husband. I order the same thing, from the same menu, from the same restaurant every time. I'm a wife who homeschools three growing young men, a preacher, worship leader, creative director, writer who works from home, a copastor of our house church, and wearer of a lot of different hats on staff at a pioneering church that's building an airplane in flight. I don't have time or space for additives or comparisons.

The Law doesn't save or give life. It's not about religious rule-keeping. It's not about adding another formula to your already extensive collection. If anything, it's about taking away the additives and getting back to the simplicity of the gospel. Jesus really IS enough. We just haven't stopped the ministry wheel long enough to remember only ONE THING was ever really needed.

> **JESUS REALLY IS ENOUGH. WE JUST HAVEN'T STOPPED THE MINISTRY WHEEL LONG ENOUGH TO REMEMBER THAT ONLY ONE THING WAS EVER REALLY NEEDED.**

This book is also not a message about rebellion rooted in church hurt. If you're looking for divisive dialogue, you won't find it here. Many voices preach unhealed narratives from their pain and offense—some of which sounds like life, but tested to Scripture is really death and division.

The Holy Spirit isn't in the habit of speaking words that contradict the Word. This isn't a gospel of self-help and the idolization of feelings. I prayerfully hope this message is coming from the overflowing river of my own journey toward healing. It's not an invitation to attack other people's ministries, methods, or mindsets. It isn't a call to judge motives or to debate forms and styles. It's only about allowing the Lord to sift our OWN hearts and motives. We're laying ourselves under His microscope—not holding others down under our faulty filters. There's no good fruit that comes from detail mining with the accuser. When people we've propped up fail, if any other compulsion besides prayer, empathy, and repentance crosses our minds, maybe we're part of the problem.

There is no oil on who we pretend to be. Let me put it another way. We only have authority over the battles we've actually won, not the battles we've *pretended* to win. When pastors are preaching "more famous" (it feels gross even saying that), peoples sermons word for word without crediting the source, and they're pretending the revelation came directly from God to appear relevant to their congregations, we need to check our egos. Or better yet, we need to let God heal the insecurity that is driving our ministries to the brink of narcissism.

I want to be gentle and clear here because, obviously, imposter syndrome is a real problem in the church, causing many to stay frozen in fear on the shoreline. I'm not talking about feeling inadequate because someone with more influence said it first or better or had more likes. I'm talking about being the bride before the wedding, asking to borrow oil because she didn't buy any for herself. That's the problem. It's wanting the fruit of intimacy with Jesus without the actual act of intimacy.

A lot of voices have been muzzled and shut down by internal comparison. Social media has both escalated the problem (because of our own poor boundaries) and helped take the message of Jesus farther than we could ever imagine. It's not the tool's fault the house falls apart. It's the builder who used it wrong.

It's knowing when to turn all the other voices and conflicting messages off and just lean into His voice. In the river of God, there is joy that can't be manufactured. His yoke is easy, and His burden is light. Striving and comparison drown under the waves of His unfathomable love and mercy. Every other voice has to bow to His.

We can copy a formula for so long we forsake our own unique purposes, personalities, gifts, and creative expressions. And the world isn't better off for it. All inspiration ultimately comes from the Holy Spirit and Scripture. Recycled oil from man is never a pleasant experience. It's like maggoty manna. We need FRESH oil. The supply is endless and we always have access. We're far too content with hit-or-miss encounters when Jesus taught us to need and ask for *daily* bread.

God only made one you, and you uniquely reflect Him in a way nobody else can. This is how we push back the gates of hell. This is how we bring His kingdom to earth. This is how rivers of revival roll into our homes and flood the streets of our cities. He can raise up someone else to take over your assignment but nobody else can fill the shoes of being YOU.

Just because someone else is speaking on any particular subject doesn't disqualify you from adding your voice to the conversation. Your voice matters. The oil of your intimacy with Jesus matters. One drop can do more than years of networking and ladder climbing. But at the end of the day, His voice always matters more.

AT THE END OF THE DAY, HIS VOICE ALWAYS MATTERS MORE.

This is an invitation for the Ecclesia to step back into kingdom alignment. To trade our church mindsets for kingdom ones. To deal with our mixture, politics, and the things we've built to attract crowds that have possibly stopped attracting heaven. The things we do to point people to Jesus but are actually only pointing them to our brand.

It's especially an invitation to purity. To be power washed by the blood and set free from the places we've gotten our identities entangled in a web of striving for approval instead of rooted in deep wells of Father God acceptance. To see our true condition so we can be effective ministers of the gospel of Jesus Christ:

> "You are blind to your evil. Shouldn't the one who cleans the outside also be concerned with cleaning the inside? You need to have more than clean dishes; you need clean hearts! "Great sorrow awaits you religious scholars and Pharisees—frauds and imposters! You are nothing more than tombs painted over with white paint—tombs that look shining and beautiful on the outside but filled with rotting corpses on the inside. Outwardly you masquerade as righteous people, but inside your hearts you are full of hypocrisy and lawlessness." —Matthew 23:26-28 (TPT)

We have a powerful river living inside of us. It's moving heavy stone, shifting bedrock, carving through rock, and shaping the path laid before us. If we feel dry, it's not because the Living Water has run out. It's because the additives have blocked the flow of the river. All the things we add to make the outside of the cup look clean have to go. All the things we add and take away to make people more comfortable with Jesus in our church services must go. This riverbed isn't meant to dry up. It's meant to flow until He comes. You're invited into the river.

Revival and reformation have become trending buzzwords since 2020, but there's a real flowing river that's on the move and lives are being transformed by it. The Lord wants us to feel the weight of the words we speak and to understand His heart behind the language He releases over a generation. He wants to define the meaning of those words. That means our experiences are not attaching meaning to His word. The word He speaks is attaching meaning to our experiences. This oil isn't cheap. It's costly. We can slap revival on our t-shirts, but the power isn't in our presentation. It's in the person of Jesus transforming the inside. I have a closet full of revival t-shirts too, but those t-shirts won't lead anyone to Jesus if it's not also lived out in the fruit of my life.

The other day, I was busy paying for gas on our way to a ministry event and was wearing a hat that said, "The Jesus Way." The man behind the counter stopped me and said, "You know what Jesus would have you do?"

I wasn't rude, just rushing and surprised by the question. I responded with a question: "Love people?"

He replied, "Jesus would have you smile."

It was a beautiful reminder that loving God and loving people looks like something and requires something. It can't just be language with no substance.

We are leading people to the river of God's love. To wild, untamable rivers of joy. Joy is a person named Jesus. Joy is our weapon. It's our strength. This river isn't boring and stoic and somber.

Weeping lasts for the night, but JOY comes in the morning. We take ourselves way too seriously sometimes and forget that we're connected to a river of gladness. In the words of my new friend from the gas station, "Jesus would have you smile again."

> There is a river whose streams make glad the city of God, the holy place where the Most High dwells. God is within her, she will not fall; God will help her at break of day. —Psalm 46:4-5 (NIV)

Ministry can be painful, but it's also joyful. You can't experience that level of joy outside of Christ and the church. If we're not careful, the buzz words we preach and slap on our clothes not actually lived out in the fruit of our lives will only cheapen the way people experience Him through us. Following Jesus looks like something. But sometimes wearing "The Jesus Way" hat is easier than actually *going* His way.

This is what the Holy Spirit wants to correct in our ministries. The gap between our private life and our public presentation. You can put lipstick on a pig, but it's still going to end up as bacon. Maybe that's a bad metaphor—because we love our bacon. Or maybe it's an accurate metaphor because we also love to call hype "revival," talent "anointing," and popularity "healthy."

Revival and emotionalism are two vastly different things with measurable differences. Emotion may be a beautiful expression of revival, but it's certainly not the whole substance of it. True revival is more substantial than weepy altars. Jesus is revival. When we pray for revival or reformation, we're praying for Jesus to come and transform us *personally*. We are asking for lasting change. Not hype.

A British Evangelist born in the 1800's by the name of Gipsy Smith said it best. When asked how to start a revival he answered: "Go home, lock yourself in your room, kneel down in the middle of your floor. Draw a chalk mark all around yourself and ask God to start the revival inside that chalk mark. When He has answered your prayer, the revival will be on." Draw a circle around yourself. That's where revival begins. Jesus plus additives is mixture, and revival starts with returning to the fear of the Lord and repenting for the mixture we've allowed in.

JESUS PLUS ADDITIVES IS MIXTURE, AND REVIVAL STARTS WITH RETURNING TO THE FEAR OF THE LORD AND REPENTING FOR THE MIXTURE WE'VE ALLOWED IN.

Powerful gifts without the fear of the Lord is a house built on sinking sand. I've learned the hard way not to ask the Lord to take me someplace my character can't keep me. "Search me, O God!" from Psalm 139:23 (NLT) has become a daily prayer. Character is the container for everything precious the Lord has asked you to carry. If you want to go the distance, the fear of the Lord is your very best friend. None of us is perfect, and Jesus doesn't expect us to be. He can redeem every part of our stories. But taking your calling lightly is costly. Mixture and compromise block the flow of the river. Humility, repentance, and the fear of the Lord restore that flow.

Sometimes, what we think is revival is really only a trickle in the bucket. Comfort and consumerism are the last things we want to idolize during true revival. We want the transformation happening on the inside to move out and transform the culture around us. That starts with being honest about what revival is NOT.

REVIVAL IS NOT:
- Hype
- Arrogance
- A Buzz Word to Prop Up Our Ego
- Emotionalism
- Screaming Sermons
- Loud Prayers
- Goosebumps
- Flawless Worship Sets
- Weepy Altars
- Good Music
- Saints Gathered
- Demons Flying Out of People
- Your Next Social Media Campaign

We are fire stewards—not fire starters. He is the flame. Real revival doesn't need announced any more than a river needs announced. You know it when you see it. It's about the heart, not the show. The fruit, not the form. It's hearts coming into true repentance and getting real freedom and families and culture being transformed from the overflow. If you're in the midst of a personal revival, by the end of it, your life will not look the same. Your desires won't be the same. Your appetites will change.

If it's just a good Sunday, that's okay too. We don't need to slap a revival sticker on everything for the sake of sounding spiritual or significant. We often conflate appearance with God's approval. But manufacturing revival is the work of the enemy who is a created being. He doesn't create, and he isn't creative. He counterfeits. Be careful that you're not seeking *counterfeit* revival. Real revival will bring about lasting change and ongoing discipleship. It will be marked by genuine repentance. There is measurable fruit. Hearts will encounter the love of God. Dead things will come alive. The real thing will quickly expose the areas we wrestle with trying to control the river. The church belongs to Christ. She always has. She always will.

MANUFACTURING REVIVAL IS THE WORK OF THE ENEMY WHO IS A CREATED BEING. HE DOESN'T CREATE, AND HE ISN'T CREATIVE. HE COUNTERFEITS. BE CAREFUL THAT YOU'RE NOT SEEKING COUNTERFEIT REVIVAL.

For everything God has ever spoken into existence, the enemy has a counterfeit manifestation, hoping our senses will be too dull to discern the difference. He masquerades as an angel of light, not a red guy with a pitchfork. He comes packaged in a thousand tiny compromises cloaked in things that prop up our identity. Tiny deaths wrapped in promises of pleasure. He can even convince us we're living in fullness when we're not. He can even manufacture a river, and if we haven't experienced the real thing, it's hard to discern the difference.

Counterfeit fruit is lulling the church to sleep, and it's wake-up time bride. We can't fake fruit, and our bowls of wax fruit won't satisfy a world starving for a real encounter with Jesus. God is calling us to TASTE AND SEE. The fruit of loving Him has a taste.

Sometimes, we try to take shortcuts and just add MORE bowls of fake fruit instead of staying connected to the Source for the real thing. And in the words of Nacho Libre, "Those eggs were a lie, Steven. They gave me no eagle powers! They gave me no nutrients!"[1] Paul writes Timothy a letter sharing some of the characteristics of the last days. This is a warning for the days we're living in:

> But you need to be aware that in the final days the culture of society will become extremely fierce. People will be self-centered lovers of themselves and obsessed with money. They will boast of great things as they strut around in their arrogant pride and mock all that is right. They will ignore their own families. They will be ungrateful and ungodly. They will become addicted to hateful and malicious slander. Slaves to their desires, they will be ferocious, belligerent haters of what is good and right. With brutal treachery, they will act without restraint, bigoted and wrapped in clouds of their conceit. They will

---

1 *Nacho Libre*, directed by Jared Hess (2006; Hollywood, CA: Paramount Pictures), 00:45:24 in the Blu-ray version.

> find their delight in the pleasures of this world more than the pleasures of the loving God. They may pretend to have a respect for God, but in reality they want nothing to do with God's power. Stay away from people like these! —2 Timothy 3:1-5 (TPT)

Jesus is the only Hero. We have to stay close to Him to navigate these days. The way He can shift a heart is astonishing. From dark to light. From wrong to right. From death to life. It's not a partial work. It's a "total reformation of how we think" (Romans 12:2, TPT). Paul went from hunting and murdering the church to laying down his life for the very gospel He once persecuted. I went from building tiny kingdoms to begging God to blow them all apart. That's what happens when you taste and see the real thing. It ruins you to lesser lovers.

I can build a lot of amazing things in my flesh, but I found out the hard way that what you build in the flesh, you will burn yourself out trying to sustain in the flesh: "For what does it profit a man to gain the whole world and forfeit his soul?" (Mark 8:36, ESV) What does it profit us to gain followers and lose faith or to have full bank accounts and prodigal children? What does it profit us to preach heaven on Sunday and live under the influence of hell on Monday or to keep secrets that are killing us? What does it profit us to win arguments but lose relationships? The things that have no profit need to go. Our love for Jesus and His church will deepen in the metamorphosis, and our character will be strong enough to hold what heaven wants to release over our lives.

You will not find any church growth recipes here—only an invitation to topple our ivory towers. To undo what needs undoing. To throw out the wax fruit and cultivate the real thing. To trade our formulas for flowing rivers. I'm truly concerned and convicted that the church would rather have a magic formula for growth than Jesus walking in the room rearranging things, making a whip, and flipping our tables. "Zeal for your house consumes me." (Psalms 69:9) I believe it still consumes Him. The problem is that it doesn't always consume us. We need His cleansing more than ever. Conviction and the fear of the Lord are gifts to our souls. Refining and sanctification are a lifelong journey. We never fully arrive this side of heaven. Wherever you are on the journey, there is always more room for growth and transformation.

Every detail of how this book was birthed into reality has been touched by divine design. Cultivated in the tender broken-up soil of my own pain, disappointment, and deliverance. The seed buried out of sight in darkness dies so something beautiful and fruitful can be born. Turns out that the Lord knows how to turn the crap we walk through into fantastic fertilizer for His purposes to grow. What has felt dead in you is maybe just a seed that's going to bring nourishment to many.

TURNS OUT THAT THE LORD KNOWS HOW TO TURN THE CRAP WE WALK THROUGH INTO FANTASTIC FERTILIZER FOR HIS PURPOSES TO GROW.

Those same rivers of joy flowing from the throne of God are also flowing inside of you. Heaven is waiting in eager expectation to see the sons and daughters of God revealed. To shake off the rejection of man and step into the river to become who He's always known we could be. We were never made to function like mass-marketed ministry machines. You're not a cog in the wheel, keeping the day-to-day activity of the kingdom spinning. You're a child of the living God—not an employed professional Christian.

Maybe it's time to remove functionality and efficiency from the throne of our hearts and the main topics of our meetings and place Jesus back where He belongs in the order of things. He never intended for our families or our purity to be casualties of war in the pursuit of revival. Real moves of God can't be manufactured. So much happens when the only strategy we have left is giving Jesus back His hammer.

I'm just one voice in a sea of voices crying out in the wilderness: "Make the way for the Lord. Make a straight highway in the wasteland for our King. Raise the valleys. Lower the mountains. Make the crooked places straight and the rough places smooth" (Isaiah 40:3, author paraphrase). Only a flowing river living inside us can do what Isaiah 40 prophesies.

You could close this book right now, and God will find another messenger beating the same drum and blowing the same trumpet. Since He's not changing the subject, maybe it's time we lean in really close and listen. Lord, stir a holy passion in your church to return to what You value. To love what You love. To hate what You hate. (Which is never people but the sin that ensnares them.) Our eyes are on You. Our spiritual ears are tuned to the frequency of Your voice. We hang on every word You want to say.

You can take sheep from different pastures and lead them to the same watering hole. When the different shepherds of the sheep call, the sheep are so familiar with their own shepherd's voice that they sort themselves out. This is what it means when Jesus says in John 10:27 (NIV), "My sheep listen to my voice; I know them and they follow me."

It's really time we sort some stuff out, church. In the end, Christ will sort us *all* out. Are we following cultural trends or the Good Shepherd of our souls? It's one thing to be an influencer in this world but quite another to be influenced by it and to replicate the same value systems when Scripture tells us not to. What are we doing here? The Bible says, "Choose this day" (Joshua 24:15, ESV). I don't think God asks this of us because He's insecure. I think He asks us to choose because we will get torn apart trying to live divided between two kingdoms.

I was a flutist and the drum major for my high school marching band. This always comes as a surprise to the people who know me because I have a gentle voice and don't come across as the barking-out-orders type. I learned the art of marching backward for miles in rain, snow, ice, and heat—me and my little whistle, not always seeing where I was going while directing a group of musicians to move forward in unison and enthusiasm.

God spoke another word to me at the end of 2019 during that difficult season of grief and transition, moving our family across the country to basically start over in a new unfamiliar land. He said, *This is my holy reset.* I thought it was a personal word for the season our family was stepping into, but it turned out to be a *global* reset for the church. I liken it to those countless hours I spent marching backwards. I couldn't always see where I was going, but somehow, backward led me forward to the place I always belonged. It elevated my trust. Deepened my roots. Strengthened muscles that had never been used before.

MEEKNESS IS NOT WEAKNESS. IT'S YIELDED AUTHORITY.

In the kingdom, lowliness always comes before glorification. His river rushes to the low places. Jesus rode a young donkey before the white horse. Zechariah and the Gospels describe the scene as meek and lowly. I raised donkeys and am very familiar with their temperament. One day I thought it would be fun to jump on the back of my donkey Jack as a child. It started out great until he decided to run full blast ahead through a torn down barn and I was left hanging from the roof. The donkey was not the meek and lowly one in the story. Donkeys were historically ridden by royalty. Jesus is the meek one, and He calls us to a life of meekness. Without meekness, we will never yield to the river. Meekness is not weakness. It's yielded authority. Jesus could have ridden in ready for war and made a lot of people happy. There will be a day for that, but that wasn't why He came:

> He existed in the form of God, yet he gave no thought to seizing equality with God as his supreme prize.

> Instead he emptied himself of his outward glory by reducing himself to the form of a lowly servant. He became human! He humbled himself and became vulnerable, choosing to be revealed as a man and was obedient. He was a perfect example, even in his death—a criminal's death by crucifixion!
> —Philippians 2:6-8 (TPT)

Meekness is a wild stallion yielded to the voice of its Creator, submitting all that power and untamed, unbridled strength to the sound of a whisper. It doesn't need the bit and bridle to go where its Maker leads. It reminds me of a scene in *Jurassic World Dominion*.[2] Spoiler alert—if you haven't seen it, skip this next part.

There's a scene where all the dinosaurs are in danger. However, their designer has placed a microchip in each dinosaur's brain that sends gentle electromagnetic waves of information, so when there's danger, they alert the dinosaurs to gather in a safe location. The dinosaurs move without force in any direction the designers tell them to go. In the movie, you see all these terrifying giant killer dinosaurs yielding their power to follow a signal—they can't *see*—to safety.

This is meekness. We could come rolling in on all our accolades, or we can yield that authority to His rolling river, stay low, and trust the Lord to promote us according to His timing and will. The lower we go the more the oil of His presence can flow. His river rushes to the low places. Up is down. Down is up. Last is first. The least is greatest. Sometimes, the way

---

[2] *Jurassic World Dominion*, directed by Colin Trevorrow (2022; Universal City, CA: Universal Studios).

forward looks like going backwards. Back to First Love. Back to the things we did at first.

Maybe it's time we accept His invitation and step into the flowing river. Imagine this book being a slow river ride back to the garden where sin entered the story, and we stopped working *from* love and started working *for* it. It's a prophetic call to personal reformation. That begins by recognizing we have areas of our lives that are out of alignment with the plumb line of Scripture and God's original design for the church.

We live in a hyper-triggered world right now. COVID-19 unleashed horrific tragedy, and many are still healing from the trauma of it. We all know people who lost someone. Maybe that was you, and if so, I pray you feel the Father's comfort. He is close to the broken-hearted. However, another plague was unleashed on the earth long before 2020. It doesn't make many headlines, but it is the root of so much death. It's a plague called offense. It's poison in the river—an invisible trap set all around us. It's caused us to cancel people instead of working out conflicts biblically. It's caused us to hellishly reject people and call it a boundary. It's even caused us to ignore the ways our own bad behavior has wounded others.

It's hard for Jesus to trust us to host revival fire when we're keen on burning bridges. The easy road comes with unmarked tolls along the way. For one thing, many can no longer stomach the sound of different opinions, and we've started conducting ourselves like the world instead of the kingdom we belong to. Some of the sickest comments you could read on the internet are coming from *our* camp. When did we forget who the real enemy is? When did we get so hyper-focused on the speck in our brother's eye that we went blind to the plank in our own? There's nothing more cringy than a critical spirit with no self-awareness.

Offense has also caused us to label the slightest discomfort as condemnation. Bringing correction to the church is biblical, but throwing stones is not and there's a difference. We're so afraid of offending people that many even water down the truth that sets them free. Thank you to all the people holding ground and refusing to water down the gospel even when it seems like the whole earth has fallen into madness and is crying out for messages that pacify their itching ears. Thank you for staying aligned to truth and not compromising even when it's been costly. Conviction isn't a cuss word. The correction of the Lord isn't a personal attack on your ministry. His discipline isn't spiritual warfare or the enemy trying to cancel your calling. The Refiner's fire is a gift to your soul.

He prunes to promote. He cuts away to increase. It's a reward for being fruitful, and embracing it will only lead to deeper wells of freedom. God didn't reset the whole world so we could settle back into old wineskins. It may not feel like it today, but trust me, you are more resilient than you realize. Discipline only kills our flesh. If it feels like death, it's doing its job. He wants order in His house, but He also wants to kill any formula that blocks the flow of His river.

When Jesus invited me a few years ago to come away with Him into a season of hiddenness, I wish I could say I slaughtered the ox, burned the plow, and stepped into that wilderness wholeheartedly. Unfortunately, that wasn't my story. Outwardly, I complied, but internally, I went kicking and screaming. I was at war within myself. A house divided. Clinging to everything I thought I knew.

Rest didn't feel holy to me. It felt like punishment. Which is exactly why I needed it. If sitting down and just receiving from the Lord for a season feels like an attack, you probably can't see it now, but trust me—you *need* to sit down, the sooner the better. The axis of the kingdom does not rotate around our proximity to a platform.

You can probably still see my nail marks on the platforms He had to drag me off of. Losing assignments felt like losing identity because I didn't understand sonship. What I thought was punishment and fighting to preserve my calling and dreams turned out to be an invitation to embrace HIS dreams which are so much better anyway. His greatest dream was never your contribution or perfect performance. It was always walking side by side in a garden with *you*.

For every pioneer reading this who has given everything to follow Jesus, traded the flesh for the inner court, sold possessions, lost relationships, uprooted and relocated their family to new lands, and stepped into unknown seasons on just a word and a mustard seed of faith . . . who has forsaken flattery and applause and yielded to holiness and the fear of the Lord . . . who has experienced the supernatural anointing of God doing impossible things through their little laid-down lives and experienced massive attacks on their oil. . . . I'm not speaking to the lukewarm. I'm speaking to the radically abandoned, obedient, consecrated remnant with blistered hands glued to the plow. Believe me when I share this next part.

God will take your ministry to have your heart. Without hesitation. It doesn't matter how gifted, anointed, or influential you are. He will pull you out of assignments and put you into a furnace to purify your motives. He will MAKE you lie down when you exclude rest from your rhythms or when you think it depends on you more than His Spirit.

GOD WILL TAKE YOUR MINISTRY TO HAVE YOUR HEART. IT DOESN'T MATTER HOW GIFTED, ANOINTED, OR INFLUENTIAL YOU ARE.

He will not compete with the idols we make of our ministries. He will hand us over to them and let them turn to ash in our hands. He will pull apart everything we build in His name that was really a monument to our own significance. And He will do it over and over again if He has to because He loves YOU more than what you produce for Him.

His love is not passive. It is not afraid to correct and cleanse. When we start to believe the narrative that His ministry depends on us, He will quickly show us it does not. I know this because I've experienced what many of you probably have also experienced. Assignments change, but God's house still thrives without us. Praise God for that! It's not our ministry. It never was. It's always belonged to Him, and He can do whatever He wants to do with it. He could do every last bit of it without us, but He chooses to include humanity in the story—for our sake, not His.

My husband has a strong gifting of craftsmanship. When our three sons were little and wanted to help him on a project, were they actually helping Daddy, or were they *helping* Daddy? God is a loving Papa who delights in letting His kids hold a hammer, but are we actually helping, or are we *helping*? Make no mistake about it; nothing actually gets built without Him, and the things that do get built without Him are guaranteed by Scripture to fall apart.

The Father will never expose sin in our life to shame or condemn us. People may have done that to you, but He will not—ever. Those people will drown in their own condemnation and judgment. We never get better by tearing someone else down. He brings sin into the light for our wholeness and freedom. Sin flourishes in the dark. Let the light in: "Confess your sins to each other and pray for each other so that you may be healed." (James 5:16, NLT).

Until we lay down our agendas, reputations, performance, and dignity and embrace the deep and hidden work of personal revival He wants to do in us, what He wants to do through us will stay hindered by our inability to surrender to His river. This book is your invitation back to that river. To get in the boat with Jesus, lock eyes, and let His love redefine all the value and identity you've built around assignments instead of sonship. It's a call to personal reformation and kingdom alignment. A swift return to what He values. The hour is late. Lay down the toy hammers. It's not a work even our best efforts could accomplish. If God was interested in us becoming a better version of ourselves He wouldn't have sent His Son. That's far too great a sacrifice for mere self-improvement. Books can't set you free.

Conferences can't set you free. They only serve to point you in the direction of the One who can. His name is Jesus. And it's time to return to His river.

> "This is what the LORD of Heaven's Armies says:
> Return to me, and I will return to you."
> —Zechariah 1:3 (NLT)

> "Not by might, nor by power, but by my
> Spirit, says the Lord of hosts."
> —Zechariah 4:6 (ESV)

PIONEER PRAYER:

Holy Spirit, I step into the river and invite You to lead me on this journey of personal reformation. Whatever You want to pioneer through me, You first want to pioneer in me. Forgive me for the little kingdoms I've built to prop my ego on. I give You permission to topple my idols. Reveal any areas of my life where I may be out of sync with the rhythms of Your heart or out of alignment with Your Word. Bring me back into proper kingdom alignment as I say yes to all You are. Reveal any place where I've tried to control how the river rolls or traded the flowing river for formulas and flow charts. Replace the stagnant waters of religion with the flowing river of God. In Jesus's name. Amen.

THE RIVER

Pioneer Prompt:

Remove distractions. Lean into the tenderness of His voice. Is He moving you in a new direction? Ask the Lord to reveal any areas where you've been guilty of trying to control the river, afraid to jump first, or reluctant to fully surrender to His leadership in this season. Are there any holes in the sails that need to be repaired to catch the wind of His Spirit? Journal His response.

_____
_____
_____
_____
_____
_____
_____
_____
_____
_____
_____
_____
_____
_____

CHAPTER 2
The Oil Lamp

God gave me a vision a few years ago of five brides standing in a churchyard getting ready for a wedding. They looked like prostitutes. Their dresses were dirty and ripped. Their faces were covered in thick makeup—additives to cover their true condition. Jesus was jealously washing them clean with soap and water. He was weeping over their condition.

And then, in the vision, He placed a flame in each of their hands, which I discerned to represent the restoration of the Five-Fold Ministry gifts working collaboratively in the church. The brides were purified, and they carried flames of revival—gifts to equip believers for the work of the ministry.

JESUS IS EQUIPPING THE EQUIPPERS, TRAINING US TO MOVE PEOPLE FROM THE BOTTLE TO MEAT, CALLING US TO STORE OIL, REMOVING THE ADDITIVES, AND PURIFYING AND PREPARING THE BRIDE FOR A WEDDING.

Jesus is restoring apostolic houses in this hour and shifting and shaking things back to kingdom alignment. It's only painful if you resist the flow of the river. He is equipping the equippers, training us to move people from the bottle to meat, calling us to store oil, removing the additives, and purifying and preparing the bride for a wedding.

I remember at my own wedding, my husband was an hour late. (We laugh about it now.) I honestly wasn't surprised or bothered beyond concern for our hundreds of guests patiently waiting. I thought he might be running on "island time" since he's an islander, and that was sort of the inside joke before he got married and learned time management. Ha-ha!

But while I waited for the groom, there was never any doubt that he would actually come. I found out after the wedding that he was helping his family finish cooking. They were preparing a big wedding feast for the reception, and he felt bad for just leaving them behind with all that work. (Sweet guy—I'm glad I waited. Ha-ha.) But in the waiting, I was *ready* and *radiant* and *expectant* because I knew he would come. And the rest is history.

All the warfare we've experienced will one day yield and forever be silenced to the sound of "I do." Our Bridegroom King is coming. He's gone to prepare a wedding feast and a place for the bride, but rest assured. He will come. He will not delay.

Jesus is beautiful. He brings EVERYTHING back to love. Remember when all the work we did for the kingdom actually flowed from that pure place of love? All other ambitions melt away in the presence of first love. They cannot remain in a heart yielded to loving and being loved by Jesus. Love for God. Love for people. All the overflow of being beloved.

There is an unmoving fountain of peace and joy filling a radiant bride. He is the source, where the river starts and ends and starts again. A river that never dries up. A love that never forsakes. He has no flaws. He is irresistible. When He is our obsession, what else matters? What is more true than the voice of our Bridegroom? What is more beautiful than every word He speaks: "For your Maker is your Husband–the Lord of hosts is His name—and the Holy One of Israel is your Redeemer; the God of the whole earth He is called" (Isaiah 54:5, ESV).

It's time to store up oil, so we won't be caught unaware like the bridesmaids in Jesus's parable:

> Then the Kingdom of Heaven will be like ten bridesmaids who took their lamps and went to meet the bridegroom. Five of them were foolish, and five were wise. The five who were foolish didn't take enough olive oil for their lamps, but the other five were wise enough to take along extra oil. When the bridegroom was delayed, they all became drowsy and fell asleep. At midnight they were roused by the shout, "Look, the bridegroom is coming! Come out and meet him!" All the bridesmaids got up and prepared their lamps. Then the five foolish ones asked the others, "Please give us some of your oil because our lamps are going out." But the others replied, "We don't have enough for all of us. Go to a shop and buy some for yourselves." But while they were gone to buy oil, the bridegroom came. Then those who were ready went in with him to the marriage feast, and the door was locked.

> Later, when the other five bridesmaids returned, they stood outside, calling, "Lord, Lord! Open the door for us!" But he called back, "Believe me, I don't know you!" So you, too, must keep watch! For you do not know the day or hour of my return." —Matthew 25:1-13 (NLT)

Every day, we are storing something. Every day, we are worshiping something. If it's not Him, something else will quickly come in to sit on the throne that was made for Him alone because, by design, we are worshipers created to behold The Creator.

EVERY DAY, WE ARE WORSHIPING SOMETHING. IF IT'S NOT HIM, SOMETHING ELSE WILL QUICKLY COME IN TO SIT ON THE THRONE THAT WAS MADE FOR HIM ALONE BECAUSE, BY DESIGN, WE ARE WORSHIPERS CREATED TO BEHOLD THE CREATOR.

I also had a vision of workers in a field gathering grain, and there were pockets of oil scattered across the field where they would go and fill jars between gathering. And I heard the Lord say, *The harvest field is also an oil field. The harvest is a noble mission but it isn't our only mission. It's time to store up oil too—not just for today but for the wedding that's coming.* It's the oil of intimacy. Time in His presence. The presence is a real person. It's not enough to focus on the harvest if we miss Jesus. Our first assignment isn't *work*, it's love. All work flows from love.

The enemy may not have access to your inheritance, but he will always go after your attention. He doesn't want your lamp full of oil. He wants it dry. He wants your eyes focused on lesser lovers, so he places endless distractions in front of you like little foxes set loose in the vineyard of your soul. Whatever has your gaze has your worship.

The only difference between the wise and foolish virgins in the parable above was the oil of the Spirit. Those dripping and those dry. They all had a lamp, but they didn't all have the oil. You can have all the right structures and systems in place and NO oil. You can have a perfect form to hold the oil but no oil. You can do powerful things in the name of Jesus and have no oil. You can give millions to missions and have no oil. You can have gifts that minister to the masses and no oil. You can live a blameless life without compromise and have a dried-up oil lamp:

> "Not everyone who says to me, 'Lord, Lord,' will enter the kingdom of heaven, but only the one who does the will of my Father who is in heaven. Many will say to me on that day, 'Lord, Lord, did we not prophesy in your name and in your name drive out demons and in your name perform many miracles?' Then I will tell them plainly, 'I never knew you. Away from me, you evildoers!'" —Matthew 7:21-23 (NIV)

Many are buying the wrong thing at market, and in the time it takes to go to the market, the door to the wedding will already be closed. Like the ark Noah built, the door closed, and there was no getting in. It's time to know Him intimately. To return to your First Love. He is for you. He loves you. Come as you are to the table He already prepared for you. For those who have spent a lifetime with Jesus, yearn for more again.

Don't be satisfied by those hit-and-miss encounters. This ends in a wedding—not a conference. What is more important than Jesus? There are no sermons in heaven—only adoration. Store your oil. Make room for more. Whatever we magnify, we get more of. If our focus is on a move or a man, Jesus will get very small, and things that should stay small will get very big.

The Father is longing for your undivided attention. Not because He's insecure but because we're lost the moment our eyes wander away from His face. Tools and building supplies are cheap, but the oil of intimacy is costly. God never asked us to sacrifice intimacy to build His kingdom. The church God is building is a church dripping with the oil of the Holy Spirit. It's a church that is attractive to the Bridegroom.

THE FATHER IS LONGING FOR YOUR UNDIVIDED ATTENTION. NOT BECAUSE HE'S INSECURE BUT BECAUSE WE'RE LOST THE MOMENT OUR EYES WANDER AWAY FROM HIS FACE.

The closer we get to the return of Christ, don't be deceived into preparing things for Him that He didn't ask for. Or doing grand things in His name apart from intimacy. The church is turning into a bridal chamber, and the temptation and deception of the age will be to build things for Jesus—*without* Jesus. He isn't looking for employees. He is calling the bride to prepare her lamp. It's terrifying how easy it is to build things for Him without Him.

And whether you're prepared or not, He is coming, and the door is closing behind Him, and if your oil runs dry, He will say He never knew you. I don't say that in a condemning way but an urgent way. If Jesus had urgency about it two thousand years ago how much closer are we now to seeing Him rip open the eastern sky and come back for what belongs to Him?

There is a great sifting happening in the church between the ready and the unready. They were all brides, but they weren't all ready. They fell asleep to what mattered most. There's a line being drawn in the sand right now. God's not drawing the line; our daily choices are! What we choose to look at is. What we choose to build and store is. There is a fence called lukewarm that makes God want to spit us out of His mouth. It's time to pick a kingdom because He is shaking everything that can be shaken until we do.

He sees the places where we're wrestling to hold onto something that is dead. It needed to die. He paid for that funeral. He doesn't plan on resurrecting it. He is drying up every other river but the one that leads home. We can't continue living torn between two kingdoms. We will serve one and hate the other. Let the dead things blow like chaff in the wind.

The Bridegroom is coming. Jesus promised it. Wisdom is screaming in this hour for the bride to watch and wait. The things of this world will put you to sleep. Events won't keep your lamp full. A sermon, your spouse, your church, your title, or this book won't do it for you. Yet, we habitually turn to the next thing and the next thing instead of the One Thing that's needed.

Form never filled a bridal lamp. Only a life yielded to the power and presence of the Holy Spirit will keep the lamp full. Only the anointing will break chains. The anointing resting on your life isn't for your glory or advancement. It's for breaking down strongholds and setting captives free:

> "The Spirit of the Lord is upon me, for he has anointed me to bring Good News to the poor. He has sent me to proclaim that captives will be released, that the blind will see, that the oppressed will be set free, and that the time of the Lord's favor has come."
> —Luke 4:18-19 (NLT)

Too many are filled with everything but oil and new wine. Opinions. Agendas. Marketing strategies. Politics. But no oil. The only strategy we need is intimacy. The oil of intimacy has creative solutions to a million unsolvable problems. It can break a million cycles of dysfunction and sin. You don't need another program. You need the presence. We can't afford to go another minute blinded and distracted to the hour.

You can have big clout and empty oil lamps. You can have a lot of charisma and no oil. You can fill rooms and have no oil. You can follow the best church-building models and have no oil. It's so sobering to know we can build amazing things and be locked out of our own wedding. And, my friend, it's not for us to judge. It's for us to be sober-minded regarding the condition of *our own* lamp.

We think the great toilet paper shortage of 2020 was bad; the oil shortage at the time of Christ's return will be devastating. It should be the main focus of every heart. The topic of every sermon. It should keep us awake at night. It should burden us to pray and see others snatched from the fires and led to the One who saves. It's time to know the season and return to our First Love.

We can be as gifted as they come, but without the oil of His presence resting on our lives, at best, we'll fill stadiums, and at worst, everyone will walk out as bound as when they walked in. Because it's not our gifting that sets people free; it's the anointing of God that breaks yokes of oppression: "And it shall come to pass in that day, that his burden shall be taken away from off thy shoulder, and his yoke from off thy neck, and the yoke shall be destroyed because of the anointing" (Isaiah 10:27, KJV).

To be anointed by God is to be consecrated—set apart for a unique and holy purpose. That's complicated when we care more about being famous. Nobody wants to address the heart when they're benefiting from the talent. The world is filled with more giftedness than at any other time in human history. Yet there are more in bondage, oppression, and confusion than there have ever been. I propose more giftedness won't solve the problem. We need more anointing.

As a family, we have been called to raise consecrated children from before they were born. You'd be surprised how many believers get upset over something that heaven values so deeply. How many people question our decisions as parents to not participate in certain things? Consecration should be peculiar to the world, but what's concerning is when it starts being peculiar to the church. When the church celebrates the very things that grieve the Spirit and are disparaging toward consecration, we've lost the fear of the Lord.

God's piercing gaze is searching the earth for marked sons and daughters set aside to be used as vessels of honor. Marked lovers who understand and who value what the Lord values. We cannot value what the Lord values and not also be grieved by the things that grieve Him because "God has called us to live holy lives, not impure lives" (1 Thessalonians 4:7, NLT).

We can't buy or borrow the anointing. Simon the Sorcerer tried to use money to buy the anointing in Acts 8:19 (NLT): "Let me have this power too." Sometimes, we want someone else's oil without also experiencing the crushing that pressed it out of them. Oil has two main ingredients: crushing and intimacy. The two things we avoid the most. Peter's response reflects God's heart when we want gifts without intimacy:

> "May your money be destroyed with you for thinking God's gift can be bought! You can have no part in this, for your heart is not right with God. Repent of your wickedness and pray to the Lord. Perhaps he will forgive your evil thoughts, for I can see that you are full of bitter jealousy and are held captive by sin."
> —Acts 8:20-23 (NLT)

The oil is not safe with anyone who is not also willing to be a consecrated container. Only praying for the anointing to look impressive and important is the same sin Peter rebuked in Simon. The only difference is that Simon's spirit is not only tolerated in our churches today but also often celebrated as a virtue called vision. Heaven just calls it selfish ambition.

> **GOD WEIGHS OUR MOTIVES CAREFULLY. HE IS TOO KIND OF A FATHER TO GIVE US SOMETHING THAT WILL DESTROY US.**

Absalom was pretty ambitious too. Anytime we try to take a throne that's not ours to take and get a legitimate gift through illegitimate means, we've stepped into rebellion. God weighs our motives carefully. He is too kind of a Father to give us something that will destroy us. None of us will arrive at perfection's shores this side of eternity, but this consecrated lifestyle requires selfish ambition and pride to be crushed in us so the things of God can live in us. It requires us to walk with the following:

» Humility—Luke 14:11
» Meekness—Matthew 5:5
» Righteousness—Romans 6:13
» Purity—Malachi 3:2
» Oil—Psalm 92:10

We walk in these qualities, we do not worship them. Jesus is the focus. Intimacy is the goal. He doesn't pour oil from a distance: "Your anointing has made me strong and mighty.

You've empowered my life for triumph by pouring fresh oil over me" (Psalm 92:10, TPT).

Our Bridegroom King is coming back for a pure and readied bride. That doesn't point to a kingdom of striving. It points to a kingdom of relationship, intimacy, connection, and delight. He is jealous over His bride. He is cleansing her from mixture, washing away the additives, and doing a deep and lasting work of preparation. In most any other context, a bride with two lovers would be considered an adulterer. In the church, we sometimes like to call it being relevant.

Judas came to Jesus with an agenda. Mary came with oil. Pour your oil. It offends wicked agendas. Maybe the resistance you feel isn't about you; maybe it's that oil you're bringing to Jesus. Maybe it exposes the dry hearts of others. Keep pouring! It's not for man. Keep pouring out what pleases God. He is searching for hearts who will protect what's precious to Him. He is searching for Ezras and Nehemiahs—restorers and protectors of pure worship.

Pride turns pure worship into an industry of striving, performing, and self-glorification. The enemy is an expert at distraction. He gets us to focus on our platforms so we forget a wedding is coming and about the oil we've been called to store. He is jealous of Levites who choose the oil of intimacy that he forfeited through pride and rebellion. There is a war on your oil, and the enemy would love for you to forget it.

The enemy also seeks to shut down the pure voices of the pioneers calling the bride to prepare for the wedding. I have come to call this spirit "The Muzzler" because its agenda has been to muzzle my voice since I was in my mother's womb and many moments since. The Lion of the Tribe of Judah muzzles the muzzler with the sound of His holy roar. His roar is removing the gag order assigned to your voice. So open your mouth, bride, and pour your oil.

Religion always seeks to make very simple things complicated. This reformation is a return to simplicity. Feel the freedom and permission that come with that. Maybe in your next staff meeting, instead of looking for things to add, look at the things the Holy Spirit may be gently wanting to strip back. Instead of adding more to your plate as a family, the Lord is inviting you to reevaluate your priorities. Maybe He wants to declutter the chaos so when it's time to go, your shoulders aren't weighed down by old dusty mantles. Your feet aren't tethered to outdated assignments.

You are invited to the Lord's table to feast on intimacy. We are battling principalities, powers, rulers of darkness, and spiritual wickedness in high places. Your battle is not with a man, person, or organization but with a spirit who is scared to death for you to open your mouth and is constantly putting comparisons before you, so you'll stay too busy to store oil. I suggest we follow John's advice:

> So I counsel you to purchase gold perfected by fire, so that you can be truly rich. Purchase a white garment to cover and clothe your shameful Adam-nakedness. Purchase eye salve to be placed over your eyes so that you can truly see. All those I dearly love I unmask and train. So repent and be eager to pursue what is right. Behold, I'm standing at the door, knocking. If your heart is open to hear my voice and you open

the door within, I will come in to you and feast with you, and you will feast with me. And to the one who conquers I will give the privilege of sitting with me on my throne, just as I conquered and sat down with my Father on his throne. The one whose heart is open let him listen carefully to what the Spirit is saying now to the churches. —Revelation 3:18-22 (TPT)

Your oil carries breakthrough and healing for nations and neighbors. It's costly. It carries purity. It's a full feast. The enemy tried to cut it off at the Source, but it's delivery day, and you're coming out of the fire refined and purified. You've been trained in the flames, and they increased the value of your oil. Others will be nourished from its overflow.

The oil you store shatters glass ceilings and walls, blocking you from your destiny—and not only you but those who will come after you. The oil you are storing causes giants to fall and towers to topple. But YOU will not be the breaker of these ceilings and walls or the toppler of these towers! This breakthrough won't come about through human striving or effort. The Breaker alone will accomplish this breaking:

> "The breaker [the Messiah, who opens the way] shall go up before them [liberating them]. They will break out, pass through the gate and go out; So their King goes on before them, The Lord at their head."
> —Micah 2:13 (AMP)

YOU HAVE A BREAKER—a Defender who goes ahead of you and breaks open the way that was shut. His name is King Jesus. You WILL pass through! You WILL rise! I prophesy oily days ahead of you! There is a purity to your posture that is unlocking promotion. Promotion doesn't come from the north, south, east, or west. Promotion comes from the hand of the Lord. It's His kindness. It's His favor.

You didn't return the spears they hurled. You didn't wear that ill-fitting armor into battle, even if it did come from kings. You didn't seek revenge on those who sought to suppress and supplant you. You didn't deserve it, but God saw it all, and He exalts the humble and humbles the proud.

Your enemies promoted you. Their accusations matured you. Their rejection made space for the favor of the Lord. Their absence made space for the increase of His hand. The crushing made your oil pure. God never once has wasted a painful season. Turning ash piles into cathedrals is just another Tuesday for Him. Nothing is impossible for God. That's not cliché. That is the reality of the kingdom you belong to.

The enemy will always look for ways to attach shame to your oil. It will be too much for some. Not enough for others. But in doing so, he also runs the risk of showing his hand because every time he attacks your strength, he inadvertently exposes his weakness. He speaks a language of shame and slander, but Jesus doesn't stop Mary from bringing her oil even when some of his own circle tried to shut it down. She chose to bring the one thing He was actually there for.

Even as you read this, I believe Christ is healing deep places of rejection in some of you. Redeeming lost time and leading you into the land you've been called to occupy. He is healing places where you were told to put your oil away and chased out of a promise. He's healing places where others have felt threatened by your anointing and dismissed it as wasteful to cover up their own dry hearts. You don't have to receive one single arrow of rejection or label that didn't come from the Lord. We break agreement with those lies in the name of Jesus and partner with the true report of heaven.

IF YOU WANT TO FOLLOW CHRIST, YOU CANNOT FEAR FAILURE AND REJECTION.

A word of caution: You won't always get it right. You'll fumble and make mistakes. You'll mishear. You'll mess up. You'll be corrected—maybe even publicly. You'll be tempted to never be vulnerable again. To shut down oil production. To morph into a yes-man who just goes with the flow of the room. To tip-toe around the river instead of diving head first. If you want to follow Christ, you cannot fear failure and rejection.

You were not the problem you were made to think you were, but you're about to be a big problem for hell. The enemy didn't realize that you were growing in the dark. He didn't realize what was walking out of that fire. If he had known the pressure and pain were posturing your heart to be a purified container for holding glory, he never would have put his mouth against you. Recompense is coming, my friend, hang on. Wait for the Lord. You're walking out with more than what walked out on you. What applied to King David applies to you too: "You prepare a table before me in the presence of my enemies. You anoint my head with oil; my cup overflows (Psalms 23:5, NIV).

If the enemy had only known that the pit he had you thrown into would purge your character and prepare you for the dreams of God. That instead of bitterness, you would drink a cup of cheer. Instead of retaliation, you would choose the way of peace. If he had known that the rejection of man would lead you to the full acceptance of the Father. That the closed door would lead to new doors, new land, and the favor of the Lord. That the slander would be your stepping stone. If he only knew then what he surely knows now, he would have chosen a different pioneer to attack.

God found David in a field when his own father didn't think he was worth being an option in the lineup to be king. He found him because He never lost him to begin with. God sees you cultivating good things in secret. He knows exactly where to find you when it's time, but His time is never the same as ours.

God is doing the same thing for you that He did for Joseph: "God's promise to Joseph purged his character until it was time for his dreams to come true" (Psalms 105:19, TPT). He found Joseph in a pit when his own brothers would rather he be dead than live another minute under the shadow of his anointing. He found him again in prison when his character had been assassinated. God never wastes a perfectly good pit. Ten out of ten times, He will use it to prepare you for a mighty big destiny if you steward your pit well. I've often felt like Joseph. But keep rejection in perspective. Without rejection, there wouldn't be a resurrection. God is using it to position you to help the very people who hurt you.

> **TEN OUT OF TEN TIMES, HE WILL USE IT TO PREPARE YOU FOR A MIGHTY BIG DESTINY IF YOU STEWARD YOUR PIT WELL.**

To the one reading this who is standing in the middle of the fight of your life. The one feeling a desperate thirst for retaliation. To the one pining to set the record straight regarding how they treated you and what really happened. It wasn't right. Maybe it really was political. Maybe it was even spiritually abusive toward you and your family. Maybe your discernment was right the whole time. I'm so sorry. I pray every bit of it is brought to light and that bad behavior is dealt with biblically. I pray you find the support and healing needed to move forward.

But may I gently encourage you that two wrongs never have made anything right. Move humbly and confidently in the opposite spirit of what's warring against you. God resists the proud but gives grace to the humble. Don't own things that aren't yours to own, but also don't get caught up in the second-heaven swirl of repaying evil with evil. You don't need to defend your reputation. The fruit of your life will be your defense. The people meant to stay . . . will.

Don't sin in your anger against the injustice of what was done against you. The battle belongs to the Lord. You can't control what happened, but you can keep your side of the street clear from the wreckage of it. Don't let it pollute your oil. Nothing corrupts the purity of our oil like bitterness. You're called to pioneer; you can't climb to new heights and hold on to unforgiveness.

Sometimes, the most dangerous offense is the offense we actually feel entitled to because a legitimate wrong was done against us. It's not an assumption. A very real evil came to steal, kill, and destroy. You truly were violated. Something was robbed from your house. Trust was broken. Whatever the packaging, offense is always poison. Let it go. Grieve what was lost, shake off the dust, and keep moving. Onward and upward, pioneers.

Don't allow that injustice to continue robbing years of your life. Don't empower it to keep sabotaging future relationships and possibilities. He works all things together for good for those who love God and whom He has called. In my thickest Southern girl accent, "If it ain't good, He ain't done."

Honor, holiness, humility, and the fear of the Lord are the way forward. These qualities protect the purity of your oil. They shield your heart from pollutants. The enemy has power for now, but he doesn't have authority. It's important to know there is a difference. Jesus has ALL authority in heaven and on the earth, and He gave that authority to you. "All authority" means there's none left over for the enemy.

Don't give up now. You're so close to breakthrough. Stay where Jesus is, and go where He goes. Posture your heart in purity, and fill your lips with praise. Pour your oil. Every last drop. Whether you're invited to the room or not, whether people think it's wasteful or tactful or weird or not, boldly pour it all out at the feet of Jesus. It is costly oil, and He is worth the cost. He is worth what He asks for. He gave His life. The least we can do is give up our dignity.

Second Samuel 6:16 (NLT) describes what happens when a person won't surrender their dignity:

> When the ark of the Lord entered the City of David, Michal, the daughter of Saul, looked down from her window. When she saw King David leaping and dancing before the Lord, she was filled with contempt for him.

Michal refused to become undignified before the Lord. What's worse is she mocked her husband's worship. The river in you will always expose the dry places in others. The river in you will always expose the hands clinging to old wineskins. You better know people would rather shut down the flow of your river any day than have to address their own dryness. Some may tell you that the best use of your oil is to water it down to the level of understanding in a room. We don't take our worship down—ever. We call the room up. They'll get there eventually, or they'll find another room with leaders willing to cater to consumers.

YOU DON'T REALIZE HOW DEAD SOMETHING IS UNTIL YOU EXPERIENCE TRUE LIFE.

You don't realize how dead something is until you experience true life. Michal was filled with contempt for David's oil. She didn't think it was even worthy of consideration or respect; she was disgusted by his lack of shame. Did David apologize? Did

David read the room and tone it down? Was David hindered whatsoever by the fear of man? Let's find out:

> David retorted to Michal, "I was dancing before the Lord, who chose me above your father and all his family! He appointed me as the leader of Israel, the people of the Lord, so I celebrate before the Lord. Yes, and I am willing to look even more foolish than this, even to be humiliated in my own eyes! But those servant girls you mentioned will indeed think I am distinguished!" So Michal, the daughter of Saul, remained childless throughout her entire life.
> —2 Samuel 6:21-23 (NLT)

Michal didn't respect David's praise because she was still yoked to the past and a slave to the fear of man. It's interesting how jealousy, fear, and pride often manifest as belittling, slander, and manipulation. But David was unhindered. Michal didn't experience David's victory, and he wasn't going to stop to make sure she'd be okay with his praise. He wasn't trying to make her comfortable; he was trying to glorify God. He didn't think to himself, *Do you think Michal would be offended if I celebrate since she's Saul's daughter? Maybe it's in poor taste. Maybe I should just celebrate quietly in my spirit.*

Where are the wild ones with holy chutzpah who haven't forgotten that faith without action is dead? The Levites with the guts to shake off all the cutting, belittling, backbiting slander in the room to bring God the glory He's worthy of? Where are the pioneers who leave normal to follow a cloud? Where are the undignified Davids willing to go even lower to lift the King high? It's time to rise up and bring Jesus an offering He is worthy of, church, without checking if the room is comfortable with it first. You don't need man's permission when you have the King's.

If we only knew what some people have been rescued from, we'd let them bring their tambourines and shofars and flags and get as wild and undignified as they need to before the Lord. I'm not willing to be the lid on top of someone else's uncontainable gratitude. Maybe it's not attention-seeking behavior. Maybe it is, but are we qualified to judge that? When Judas starts judging the perfume, it's never about the perfume. It's always about hidden motives.

We need to let people weep at the altar without judgment or speculation. There may be people looking down from their high window at your praise in contempt too. Some of those people may live in your own house. You get to choose whom your offering is for, like David and Mary. If it's for God, the opinions of man won't matter.

Some people are already set on misunderstanding your oil before you ever pour it out. We don't shrink our praise to make dry hearts more comfortable. No, friends, we stay low and undignified and invite the room to come higher. We go low to bring Jesus HIGH praise.

Michal got a cup of barrenness for her contempt. Judas got rebuked. The more we stand over people criticizing their sacrifice of praise, the more barren we become spiritually. The life of a critic is a dry wasteland. Honor and unity are crucial in an atmosphere that seeks to host His presence.

> **THE HOLY SPIRIT WILL NOT REST ON A HOUSE THAT IS WICKED AND DIVIDED. WHAT'S SCARY IS THAT GIFTS CAN STILL FULLY FUNCTION, BUT THE SPIRIT HAS LEFT THE BUILDING.**

The Holy Spirit is grieved when the church operates outside of these values. He will not rest on a house that is wicked and divided. What's scary is that gifts can still fully function, but the Spirit has left the building. Paul tells us to put to rest any divisions that attempt to tear us apart and to be restored to a place of unity and harmony. It's a choreography of working in vertical and horizontal alignment.

As a person who has been both a worship leader and a pastor, I know the struggle of trying to lead a room into an encounter with Jesus and guarding the purity of our ministry to HIM first while also stewarding honor for the leader of a house and shepherding hearts into a holy encounter with the Good Shepherd. It's very important for the sake of unity and honor to submit to the pastor's vision of how a service should flow, knowing God established order and government in His house. I have found that to be even more important than the songs we pick.

This isn't a bunch of unsupervised children bulldozing over structure. If we oppose order, we oppose God. The fear of the Lord and reverence for His presence should be carefully stewarded in every house at every moment. But sometimes we've perfected a system, never stopping to ask the Holy Spirit if His oil is even on it. Ultimately, the church belongs to Jesus, and so do our services.

The rigid traditions of men can send us well on our way to grand form and efficiency while stripping us of the only Person in the room with the power to actually transform lives. Our coffee and first-time guest gifts are good but not that good. The Holy Spirit will never live in our boxes. It's exhausting trying to keep the Spirit in a box (or a set list, sermon, or order of service) He doesn't want to be in. Eventually, you're either going to bow to the fear of man or the fear of the Lord, but you cannot bow to both at the same time.

The fear of man has been a snare in my life more times than I care to confess. I've never been afraid of a stage or microphone. Just ask little Rhea, standing by herself in front of hundreds of teens at a church camp talent show, playing "Battle Hymn of the Republic" on the flute while the wind kept blowing the pages of her hymnal around!

For me, the fear of man would manifest mostly through desperately wanting love, affirmation, and approval. For many years, my value was attached to those things. But the call of God on my life has almost always been at war with that desire. Looking back, I'm fairly confident that was intentional. He was training my flesh to die. The only way to fully follow Him is to fully die to ourselves.

He'd have me pioneer paths when people didn't want change. He'd have me go first and take the deep cuts, so others wouldn't have to. At other times, He'd call me to be a reformer with a hammer, a nail, and a word. I didn't ask for the hammer, but there were things on His heart I couldn't get off mine until they were released. He'd have me speak hard truth in love when people would rather hear pleasant lies. He'd convict me to say no to things everyone else would say yes to. To draw boundary lines when people were benefiting from my lack of them. He'd have me linger just a little longer when others were ready to move on. I just wanted to pour my oil, but instead, I've been met with a lot of misunderstanding, rejection, slander, hostility, and deep cuts of betrayal. John 15:18 (NIV) tells us exactly why: "If the world hates you, keep in mind that it hated me first."

I carried the weight of those rejections in silence, which sounds noble but led to some massive fallout, missed opportunities to pour my love on Jesus, and high blood pressure. Not protecting your heart well or dealing with offense biblically leads to bitterness, and that's not beneficial for anyone because offense blocks the river and taints the oil. Stuffing pain down can even take a toll on your physical health.

Fearing the rejection of man makes pouring your oil on Jesus impossible. When I realized that people-pleasing is a pit from hell with no bottom, I got better boundaries. Not every great opportunity is from the Lord. I stopped saying yes to things Jesus was saying no to. You will lose popularity with everyone who is using you.

Boundaries will do the heavy lifting for you as they are wonderful sifters of what is true and false. I learned that the word *no* is a complete sentence and that I can respectfully decline opportunities and still be extremely valued and loved as a daughter. When His love is the only thing left defining you, hell has a hard time finding a handle to hold.

If somebody doesn't respect the boundary of my no, they are likely more concerned with my productivity than my health. One of the markers of a healthy house is maturity. They will honor your boundaries and not throw spears at you when you fail to comply with their expectations. I have been blessed to serve under many leaders who value health over performance, and those are the type of leaders who love their teams well so they last a long time.

Better boundaries will only take you so far, though. They can only solve so many issues. Some things need deliverance, inner healing, and a deep dive into what the Father speaks over your identity. Yes, even saints need to be delivered sometimes when they're being oppressed by the devil and caught in cycles of sin and webs of people-pleasing, rejection, and performing. Sometimes, saints also need counseling. Sometimes, saints don't have the mind of Christ about a topic and we need the whole counsel of God. If we removed the shame surrounding these topics, maybe fewer pastors would quit, more believers would be walking in freedom, more marriages would be restored, fewer spear-throwing Saul's would be protected and less damage would happen behind closed doors in the church.

THERE ARE ALSO TIMES WHEN THE ONLY WAY TO POUR YOUR OIL IS TO PEACEFULLY EXIT A SITUATION THAT IS STOPPING YOU.

There are also times when the only way to pour your oil is to peacefully exit a situation that is stopping you. When man stops going his direction, it creates a conflict, and we have to confront and possibly remove ourselves as honorably as possible. David honored Saul every single moment Saul was throwing spears at him. But he also jumped out of the way of the spear and removed himself from the situation. You get to determine the level of destruction and dysfunction you tolerate. Staying at the cost of your soul is too high a price. You have to decide how far you're willing to go in a direction Jesus isn't going.

It's not every Sunday that the Holy Spirit is showing up "ruining" our order of service. There have been countless times, though, I've sensed Him wanting to. Times I've wept after a service because I felt the Holy Spirit was so boxed in by a flow chart that I never wanted to lead in that atmosphere ever again. Forced to use oil reserved for the King to entertain a crowd like a prostitute.

Pastors, I beg you. I even believe the Holy Spirit is pleading with you to stop hiring performers instead of priests. Levites care about bringing excellence too. The real problem is not wanting to make people uncomfortable, and that is a sign your church is consumer-driven instead of Spirit-led.

Consumers don't understand oil. Regardless of models or methods, we should stop creating atmospheres with the goal of attracting people and build what attracts heaven because it's always been God who draws people to the Son anyway. What worked two thousand years ago . . . still works.

People are tired of the show and the gimmicks. They actually don't need everything we've been conditioned to think they do. After a few years of having church in our home, our teenage sons were at a Christian event that was explosive with hype. We thought they would love it, but on the drive home, they said, "It was nice, but I also kind of like it when it's less hyper." Essentially, what our teenagers were saying is this: "We want substance. Feed us meat."

I truly believe this is the future of the church, and they are echoing what many are searching for. Authenticity. Substance. Truth. People know when we're loving them and when we're manipulating them. The earth is groaning for something real, so they come to church and find the same entertainment they could find in the world. But we're still dragging a dead horse around pretending it's alive. Can we talk about the dead horse? Are we afraid Jesus isn't enough to keep the doors open?

Let's bring all the creative excellence to the table we can—but not for the sake of attracting people to Christ because I'm going to beat the dead horse and remind us all that it's the FATHER who leads people to the Son. Jesus says in John 6:44 that nobody would even come to Him unless the Father drew them. The apostles never performed like circus monkeys for followers. They didn't put on a concert to give Jesus a little plug at the end. They healed the sick, raised the dead, cast out demons, cleansed the lepers, and gave what they received. They went into the world and made disciples, baptized them, and taught them to follow Jesus because the Father drew them to the Son. Our productions don't do that. It's all about the Father and the Son and the Spirit.

Don't make the main thing in your church production. It's a trap. It feels like life, but the Holy Spirit isn't resting on it. As a highly creative person with a deep conviction to protect the purity of my oil, may I propose that you don't have to trade one for the other? You can have creative excellence and still protect what the Lord values. You can care about creatively reaching the lost through the arts while still prioritizing what attracts heaven. For some reason, we've settled on a lie that compartmentalizes full creative expression and full holiness. When the Holy Spirit is leading our services, we can be creative AND holy. Excellent AND sensitive to His voice. Fun AND walking in the fear of the Lord. It's both/and.

He knows the real from the manufactured. I've experienced seasons of having to stay in this strange tension between man's desire to stay seeker-sensitive and the Holy Spirit's desire to give people the One thing they actually need the most—His presence. His grace is sufficient. His truth sets men free. Some things are relinquished that can't be redeemed when we trade His presence for satisfied customers. The best sermon will always be Jesus walking into the room, and when we forget that, we're in trouble.

Over the last twenty years of ministry, I cannot even begin to tell you the war and resistance my husband and I have faced for just wanting to bring pure oil to the King and to invite others to bring their oil too. We've had to throw off Saul's armor a lot to bring Jesus gifts He's worthy of. We've had to get comfortable with being misunderstood. That unnecessary burden is the last thing Levites need on a Sunday morning when they're just trying to connect hearts to the King. It's the product of putting performers on platforms and discipling people to be consumers instead of a priesthood. Consumers come for entertainment. They come with preferences and opinions. We're called to lay all that down to follow Christ. We're called to be dead to our own agendas.

Performers perform. Levites worship. The difference in the fruit is night and day. There's no agenda or ladder they're trying to climb. There's no self-promotion, credit, or glory they're seeking for themselves. They aren't shaken by man's approval or rooted in insecurity. Those are the people you want shepherding your church from the platform. It was God who put them in that room and around that table and they know it. It's a common ache in a Levite's soul when they're asked to water down their oil or turn their worship into a performance. It's not an ache because they feel undecided about what to do. It's an ache for you.

If you're an "in spirit and in truth" kind of worshiper, you probably know this ache. Consumers love to offer feedback on your oil. Eventually, you have to decide if you're going to bow to the fear of man or to the fear of the Lord. We've been leading worship for decades in hundreds of different environments, and we love the local church and the beautiful houses we've served in, so there's no need to make assumptions as to where we've heard this feedback because it's irrelevant. Sometimes we plant seeds we never get to watch mature to full growth.

But I've had suggestions that I should not close my eyes in worship because it's not engaging with the crowd. Not to turn my back on a crowd because it disconnects with the "audience." (Performance, concert, audience, entertainment, production—that's the language of consumerism. If you're struggling with consumerism in your church, try changing the language.)

Performance < Worship
Concert < Worship
Production < Worship
Talent < Worship
Entertainment < Worship
Audience < The Church/Worshipers (You don't need a platform to be a worship leader. Lead from the back of the room.)

And while we're at it, just for good measure, let's save the applause for Jesus.

We've been mocked for our hats and holey jeans. One time, I was even told to wear bright red lipstick because it shows up better on the camera. We're so focused on man buns, skinny jeans, and our personal preferences being met we couldn't see Jesus even if He physically walked into the room. We're so enamored by talent we would put people into priestly positions to make our church look good without even caring about the conduct of their character.

We've experienced such judgment and resistance in a room from religious spirits where people refused to even worship. (Side note: If anything has the power to stop your worship, it's not worship, and your eyes aren't on Jesus.) Never compromise your worship to keep a platform or title or a room appeased. It's not worth it. If you're a leader and there's disunity and little cliques causing dissension on your team or in your house, especially in this area of worship, deal with it fast and early, or it will wreak havoc. Don't elevate talent above Christlikeness.

Priests have a mandate from God to protect the purity of worship flowing on and off the platform. Don't ask them to become performers. Allow space for them to simply love Jesus wildly and freely without having to curate a perfect stage or moment. So much life happens when we let go of control.

I've heard suggestions that we should go easy on the spontaneous songs and Spirit-filled moments because people won't be able to worship if they don't know the words. (With this logic, we are literally conditioning people to not know how to embrace the Holy Spirit's leadership.) I've also been in environments that swung the pendulum in the far opposite direction; it was open mic night with immature sheep who craved a platform. Things can get pretty wonky in both directions without pastoral oversight.

Scripture tells us to sing a new song, but there's an unspoken rule about how many new songs you can introduce in a set on a Sunday. I've been asked not to repeat the same line in a song too many times. "But what if Jesus liked that line? What if that line was releasing breakthrough in a room?" I've been blessed to serve under pastors who honor the movement of the Holy Spirit, and there's a beautiful trust and unity that happens as we navigate those moments in His presence together. There's power in our agreement as a church. We obviously want people to connect to those moments. To sing along. To contribute. But the deciding factor of how your Sunday goes should not hinge on the desires of the people or even your preparation but on the leading of the Spirit.

I'm letting you peek behind the curtain of what happens when consumerism comes to church. I'm speaking from a worship perspective, but honestly, this applies to every aspect of the church. This is the language of consumers. It's hypervigilant about catering to the people and way less concerned with what the Spirit wants. It's impossible to pioneer anything new with the Lord when everybody gets a vote on which direction to go. Get a bunch of people in rowboats and blindfold them and then have a bunch of people on the shore telling them which way to go. You're going to have a bunch of blind people going nowhere. Pastors, listen to Jesus. Follow Jesus.

We prepare with excellence. We shepherd hearts carefully into encounter, but to be the church is to be Spirit-led, not consumer-driven. I've been told the music is too loud. Told it's too quiet. Told the lights are too dark or too bright. I've had song requests placed in offering buckets. I've been told to bring more energy, that I prayed too long, or that I let worship linger a few minutes beyond the schedule.

I understand respecting people's time. It's our most precious commodity. But consumerism has come to church when we have all the space for our script and none to spare for the Lord to move outside of it. Nobody is safe from a consumer-driven church. Singing songs about Jesus and not *to* Him is the essence of a religious spirit. If we're not careful, we start to worship preferences and forms instead of God.

If there's one thing I've learned through many years of leading worship, it's that consumers do not understand oil, and they don't like it because it's the one area they can't consume. It's not for them. It's like the scene from *It's A Wonderful Life* when Mr. Potter wants to shut down the Building and Loan and George Bailey says, "I know very well what you're talking about.

You're talking about something you can't get your fingers on and it's galling you."[3] Consumers are galled when they can't control, consume, and have things catered to their preferences. This is why we need "George Baileys" to protect what's precious to the Lord. He didn't seek out that assignment but your gifts make space for you.

There's also been times when I've been a performer instead of a Priest because of my own hypocrisy and compromise. When you have gifts and a platform without character and a holy fear of the Lord that's all you *can* be until you repent and let God heal you. I conduct myself much more differently than I have in seasons past and I don't take the mantle on my shoulders and the oil and staff in my hands lightly.

Most things start pure. I didn't seek a ladder to climb or strategize myself into positions. God put me into those rooms and assignments. But things can go sideways when we don't keep our inner world on the altar or when our identity is tied to assignments instead of to Christ. Finding a safe place to get honest about your struggles could prevent a lot of heartbreak and devastation for you and for others down the road.

This is why my family and I gather in our home, worshiping as often as possible with no agenda other than pouring our love on Jesus. Sunday isn't a large enough container for all the love and gratitude He's worthy of. Performers struggle with private ministry. They can produce beautiful things without ever having to look at Jesus or how they're living privately. If Sunday is the only time you're eating a full meal, you will starve for His presence the rest of the week and you'll take on the nature of a

---

3 *It's a Wonderful Life*, directed by Frank Capra (1946; New York, NY: RKO Radio Pictures), 00:33:27.

performer. We've learned to value private inner court ministry to Jesus above outer court ministry to man. It is sacred, holy ground. And I sense the Lord is very jealous for our corporate gatherings to make His presence the main focus again. The family altar is the new wineskin for this revival—new but also as old as the garden. Before the corporate ministry machine was rolled out, family was always God's design for the church, and He's calling pioneers of His heart to return to it.

I had a dream several years ago that I was standing in a river with a bunch of people holding nets, trying to catch fish. I didn't have a net, but all the fish kept jumping out of the water and into my arms. The water was crystal clear, and I could see myself surrounded by a massive school of fish. Everyone else's nets were empty, but my arms were overflowing with fish.

When I woke up, the Lord impressed upon my heart that He doesn't need gimmicks to bring in the harvest. Nothing is more attractive than His presence. We just need to be where the fish are and hold our arms open. These are not the days for impressive nets. For too long, the focus has been on inventing more clever ways to get people into the building. (Remind me to tell you about the time I brought an indoor petting zoo into our worship center on a Sunday morning and talked about slaying sacred cows.)

Every event, we try to outdo the last and up the "wow factor" to keep people coming back, and I truly believe God sees and honors all the prayer and attention to detail put into every bit of it. There's no question about it; people get saved, but a lot of people just stay consumers. Is it worth it for the one? Absolutely. But some people won't come to a conference unless they like the speakers and worship leaders. They won't contribute. They'll leave reviews like they're food critics paid to sample Jesus.

When did the gospel become all about our preferences? So, an honest question I want to very gently ask is if God asked you to strip it down to nothing (whatever "it" is)—to not announce speakers, to not invest thousands of dollars, to make it free, to not give out gifts, or to have incentives, to scale it back to just the bare bones minimum, to not use your connections, to just invite thousands of people to come into a room where they can encounter Jesus, would you obey, or would you hesitate? Your heartfelt answer to that question might determine if consumer-driven ministry mindsets are influencing your obedience. If it's not immediate, it's not obedient.

I love creative ministry that says, "We will do anything short of sin to bring people into the kingdom." I'm wired and gifted to flow creatively. But unbridled, I can lean too far that way, toward making everything a production. As a worship and creative arts pastor, I'm all about creative strategy. But if we're elevating strategies above the oil of intimacy, we're going to produce consumers. We will never EVER mature beyond our prayer life. And we will never EVER be able to get people through the door better than the Father simply drawing them to the Son can. For good measure, let's read this one more time: "For no one can come to me unless the Father who sent me draws them to me" (John 6:44, NLT).

I have found that what you get through striving, you have to keep through striving. What you win them with is the tool you'll have to keep them with. Just as winning people to Christ through fear creates disciples of religion, winning people to Christ through performance creates—BINGO! You guessed it—consumers.

The father didn't throw a party to get his prodigal son to come home. He didn't run a social media campaign. The son came home, and then the father threw a party. The father didn't have to advertise home. The father and home were always enough by themselves for the prodigal son.

Shepherds, your heart to care for your people is beautiful. But you're not truly caring if you're not also correcting out of fear of losing sheep. We have to be willing to have hard and holy conversations with our people when these toxic mindsets are driving the mission of our church off a cliff.

If you're a pastor and you've said any of these things to your worship leaders or overheard these types of pressures being put on your worship leaders, please ask yourself a question: *Would I rather steward a mess and experience a move or avoid a mess and make an occupation out of quenching the Spirit?*

Would you rather have priests or producers and performers? Producers will always attract consumers. Priests will always attract sons. Maybe today is the day you break agreement with every vow to structures made by human hands and the mixture that's been celebrated for far too long from the platform.

PRODUCERS WILL ALWAYS ATTRACT CONSUMERS. PRIESTS WILL ALWAYS ATTRACT SONS.

If you're a believer and you've ever treated worship leaders like their job is to put on concerts for your personal entertainment, I lovingly and gently want you to ponder how God feels about that. Worship belongs to Him.

A performer is paid to keep a crowd entertained. Any person leading a room into deep, holy adoration of the Lord is called a priest, and the last thing on their mind (or yours, for that matter) should be your entertainment. We cannot continue blending the two kingdoms together as if they're the same thing. This is mixture. They couldn't be any more different. I love you, but it grieves the Holy Spirit.

God is sifting the common from the sacred. We aren't called to copy or compete with the world. We're called to give the world an encounter with heaven. It starts with keeping our own hearts on the altar and asking Jesus to sift our motives. There is a reverence and a weightiness to worship that entertainment could never manufacture. The glory cannot be marketed. God desires spirit and truth worshipers. The rudder of scripture was always meant to function WITH the sail of the Spirit. They are not separated from one another. The more we know Him, the more we are provoked to adore Him. Spirit and Truth. Truth without the Spirit is religion. Spirit without Truth is wonky spirituality. Refusing to merge the two is bondage.

Let's look at two accounts of Jesus being anointed. The first is told by John:

> Mary picked up an alabaster jar filled with nearly a liter of extremely rare and costly perfume—the purest extract of nard, and she anointed Jesus's feet. Then

she wiped them dry with her long hair. And the fragrance of the costly oil filled the house. But Judas the locksmith, Simon's son, the betrayer, spoke up and said, "What a waste! We could have sold this perfume for a fortune and given the money to the poor!" (In fact, Judas had no heart for the poor. He only said this because he was a thief and in charge of the money case. He would steal money whenever he wanted from the funds given to support Jesus' ministry.) Jesus said to Judas, "Leave her alone! She has saved it for the time of my burial. You'll always have the poor with you; but you won't always have me." —John 12:3-8 (TPT)

The second comes from Luke:

In the neighborhood there was an immoral woman of the streets, known to all to be a prostitute. When she heard about Jesus being in Simon's house, she took an exquisite flask made from alabaster, filled it with the most expensive perfume, went right into the home of the Jewish religious leader, and knelt at the feet of Jesus in front of all the guests. Broken and weeping, she covered his feet with the tears that fell from her face. She kept crying and drying his feet with her long hair. Over and over she kissed Jesus' feet. Then she opened her flask and anointed his feet with her costly perfume as an act of worship. When Simon saw what was happening, he thought, "This man can't be a true prophet. If he were really a prophet, he would know what kind of sinful woman is touching him." Jesus said, "Simon, I have a word for you." "Go ahead, Teacher. I want to hear it," he answered. "It's a story about two men who were deeply in debt. One owed the bank one hundred thousand dollars, and the other only owed ten thousand dollars. When it was obvious that neither of them would be able to repay their debts, the kind banker graciously wrote off the debts and forgave them all that they owed. Tell me, Simon, which of the two debtors would be the most thankful? Which one would love the banker most?" Simon answered, "I suppose it would be the one with the greatest debt forgiven." "You're right," Jesus agreed. Then he spoke to Simon about the woman still weeping at his feet. "Don't you see this woman kneeling here? She is doing for me what you didn't bother to do. When I entered your home as your guest, you didn't think about offering me water to wash the dust off my feet. Yet she came into your home and washed my feet with her many tears and then dried my feet with her hair. You didn't even welcome me into your home with the customary kiss of greeting, but from the moment I came in she has not stopped kissing my feet. You didn't take the time to anoint my head with fragrant oil, but she anointed my head and feet with the finest perfume. She has been forgiven of all her many sins. This is why she has shown me such extravagant love. But those who assume they have very little to be forgiven will love me very little." Then Jesus said to the woman at his feet, "All your sins are forgiven." All the dinner guests said among themselves, "Who is the one who can even forgive sins?" Then Jesus said to the woman, "Your faith in me has given you life. Now you may leave and walk in the ways of peace." —Luke 7:37-50 (TPT)

We're standing in a bridal chamber. The Bridegroom is coming for His glorious bride—holy and radiant without blemish or wrinkle. It's too late to gather the oil when the feast begins. The doors will be locked. The thought of being locked out of my own wedding is sobering. Let's keep our lamps full. This ends in a wedding.

I'VE HEARD IT SAID THAT THE HOLY SPIRIT IS LIKE HEAVEN'S WEDDING PLANNER PREPARING THE BRIDE, AND JESUS IS THE BRIDEGROOM KING PREPARING A PLACE FOR THE BRIDE.

There is a gift the Holy Spirit has given us to hope for the return of Christ. I've heard it said that the Holy Spirit is like heaven's Wedding Planner preparing the bride, and Jesus is the Bridegroom King preparing a place for the bride. Only the Father knows the day and the time of the wedding, but what if it's today? The enemy has tailor-made distractions to dull our senses—a softly sung lullaby over the bride in hopes she misses her own wedding. I can't think of a time in the history of the world when boundaries were ever more needed. When you realize distractions were designed by hell to get you to forfeit your destiny, it causes you to number your days differently.

Our daily choices expose what we worship. The mercy of Jesus is reaching down, saying, "I'm coming for a bride with fire in my eyes, jealous for My inheritance." It's spiritual adultery to love things above Him. When you know the door to your own wedding is about to open, you live differently. You lean in closer. You say no to things you should say no to and yes to the Bridegroom. You don't have time for lesser lovers. The harvest field is an oil field. Love God. Store oil. Love people and lead them to Jesus. That's what matters now. We need to bring it down to the very foundation, back to the very basics.

We don't know the hour, but we do know the season. What bride do you know who does not spend the days leading up to her wedding preparing in some way or another? This is preparation time for the church. He is coming for a spotless bride. I don't want to be a distracted bride. An offended bride. A bickering bride. A demon-oppressed bride. A sleeping bride. A compromised bride. I want His fire to make me lovely and ready. A pure bride.

Will you say yes to the invitation? I can promise you one thing. That nudge you feel pulling you into the secret place, into fasting, into intimacy, into prayer, into worship... that desire is coming from somewhere, and it's NOT the enemy. We repent of our distractions, Lord. We choose you. Nothing else matters. You really are enough, and we agree with John the Baptist:

> He is the Bridegroom, and the bride belongs to him. I am the friend of the Bridegroom who stands nearby and listens with great joy to the Bridegroom's voice. Because of his words, my joy is complete and overflows! It is necessary for him to increase and for me to decrease. —John 3:29-30 (TPT)

PIONEER PRAYER:
Jesus, you're coming back for a pure and spotless bride. Purify my motives. Help me to be a laid-down lover watching, waiting, and storing oil—not an adulterous bride full of divided affections. Search my heart and reveal areas where I've traded bridal language and intimacy for production and industry. Reveal the places where I've made it all about me. Wash me clean of mixture. Forgive me. In Jesus's name. Amen.

Pioneer Prompt:

The first ministry of every pioneer is inner court ministry to Jesus Himself. Stop building things without Him. Leave your agendas in the outer court, and simply bring your oil before the King. Return to your First Love. Soak in His presence, and journal anything He speaks to you.

_____
_____
_____
_____
_____
_____
_____
_____
_____
_____
_____
_____
_____
_____

CHAPTER 3

The Broken Ladder

冒

Growing up catholic, I knew about a good man named Jesus who died for the world. I knew even more about His mother. I knew about religion. (There are many Spirit-filled Catholics, but I was not one of them at that point in my life.) I didn't know that Jesus wanted a personal, active relationship with me until one day, as a little girl, I had what I now know to be a prophetic dream.

> **I DIDN'T KNOW THAT JESUS WANTED A PERSONAL, ACTIVE RELATIONSHIP WITH ME UNTIL ONE DAY, AS A LITTLE GIRL, I HAD WHAT I NOW KNOW TO BE A PROPHETIC DREAM.**

In the dream, I was in a deep cave with three rope ladders with wooded steps leading up and out of the cave. The only way out was up. Also in the cave were two friends from elementary school. In reality, everything they touched turned to gold. They were exceptional at everything they did. I was just sort of average. They effortlessly climbed their ladders out of the cave, and they, along with their ladders, disappeared. Then, I began to climb mine. The only dilemma was that my ladder was broken. The closer I got to the top, the more broken it was. Entire rungs were broken or missing. I was stuck. And then Jesus appeared in my dream. His eyes were smiling and full of acceptance. He lifted me out of the cave and wrapped me in an embrace that can only be described as warm, electric love piercing my whole personhood. I felt entirely whole in His arms.

Again, I wish I could say this dream immediately ushered me into a revelation of who I am in Christ. But unfortunately, I already had an identity deeply rooted in the rejection of man. It actually formed while I was still in the womb when my biological father gave my mother an ultimatum: "Abort the baby, or our relationship is over." He has his own story. There is only love and forgiveness in my heart toward him.

I'm forever grateful that wasn't a choice my mom struggled to make. She was unprepared for motherhood but was resolved and settled in her spirit to do anything humanly possible to protect the destiny resting on my still-forming body—even moving across the country from the Oregon coast to the wild rivers and woods of Missouri as a single mother with a baby. Her goal was to give me a good life surrounded by the support of a stable, loving family while she worked to provide for me.

That rejection wasn't a one-time event, though. As a fifteen-year-old I, had an opportunity to meet my biological father. I had already had a wonderful dad in my life who married my mom when I was five and adopted me. He was just about everything a little girl could dream of in a dad. But flying out to meet my biological father felt like the right thing to do as my relatives there were eager to get to know me more.

Prior to that, I had a life-changing encounter with Jesus. I had been invited to attend a little Baptist church camp in the sticks of Missouri. On July 23, 1998, I was standing in the very back of an outdoor tabernacle and a song began to play: "Just as I am, without one plea. But that thy blood was shed for me. And that Thou bid'st me come to Thee, O Lamb of God, I come! I come!"[4]

Everyone disappeared, and I felt Jesus drawing me out of the crowd and calling me to give my life to Him. I walked to the altar and never looked back. That same feeling in my dream about the broken ladder became my forever reality. I was completely whole and accepted in His arms. I wept well into the night, sitting on a bridge over a pond, thinking about God's wild love for me. Hours and hours of weeping. I didn't know it at the time, but I was experiencing deep inner healing from years of rejection. The pastor's daughter just held me, let me cry, and even blow my snotty nose into her t-shirt. If that isn't love, I don't know what is. His presence marked me that day. I celebrate it every year. And now, I share the same spiritual birthday with my youngest son, Judah. I can't think of anything better.

GOD'S PRESENCE MARKED ME THAT DAY. I CELEBRATE IT EVERY YEAR.

---

4 Charlotte Elliot, "Just As I Am," 1835, public domain.

I was so hungry for the Lord after that week at camp to be formed in a family and discipled by the Lord Himself. I'd sit at His feet for hours. If my parents were working or I couldn't catch a ride to church, I'd walk five miles into town, so I didn't miss it. (That's not an exaggeration. I actually clocked it.) I won a King James Version Bible at VBS (vacation Bible school) and immediately started memorizing it. My bedroom walls were covered in scripture that I was memorizing. His Word and His presence were my continual feast.

I'm pretty sure my family thought I was losing my mind, though. I was convinced Jesus was returning any second, and I was constantly calling classmates from our landline phone (before kids had cell phones) to scare them into the kingdom whenever the moon looked a little apocalyptic (not the best approach). I'd spend hours every day walking the countryside, going house to house sharing the gospel, and serving the needs of the elderly—by myself. Probably not recommended nowadays with the current state of the world.

Thankfully, most of my family has come to know the Lord, but I remember one day, I was literally chasing my mom around, trying to lead her to Christ before He returned, and she missed the rapture. Ha-ha! She finally locked herself in her car to get some peace and quiet. We look back now and laugh. I was a little overboard and probably needed a spiritual momma and papa to disciple me during those early years, but my heart was pure. I had the Holy Spirit, and that was enough.

All that to say, my life had been transformed, and I was excited to begin a journey toward reconciliation with my biological father and to know his side of my family. As I got off the plane with my mother, it was just as awkward and uncomfortable as one might imagine it being. I was checked out, not super accommodating to any kind of gesture, and really bound by a spirit of rejection, but I didn't know what that was at the time. I wasn't rude, just guarded. Everyone was so sweet and accommodating, but I felt like a secret scandal instead of a loved child. Like a deep wound was trying to be amended out of duty and not delight in me as a daughter.

During that trip, he spent a small fortune buying me clothes, taking me shopping, and getting me a computer for school before computers were a common household item for teenagers. After the trip, he never really talked to me again. There were many other experiences that trip that made it clear he didn't know how to be a father, and I realized his rejection was probably God's protection because it led to me being raised by a father who fathered well. Even if our earthly fathers fall short, we have a heavenly Father who covers us flawlessly.

I was grateful for the gifts and experiences, but that wasn't why I flew across the nation to meet him. I didn't grow up in that kind of luxury. We were a hard-working farming family—poor materially and far from perfect, but rich where it mattered. I learned to cultivate gratitude for simple things.

I thought things went well for our first meeting despite the walls. I was able to share my faith with him. We flew back home, and I wrote him several letters, excited to stay in touch, but he never wrote back. Years later, after I was married and had just given birth to our firstborn son, I got news from his mother (my grandmother with whom I maintained a beautifully connected relationship) that my biological father had passed away.

Years of alcoholism led him to liver disease and pneumonia. It was crushing to know I would never find the affirmation I had longed for from my own father. I'd never be enough in his eyes. I'd never be worth the effort or know why I wasn't. And that, along with many other rejections and painful situations, further sealed this deep, unspoken agreement with the lie that I have something to prove and something to earn. That simply being me was not enough. I had to somehow be better than I was. I had to work harder to be accepted. That rejection carried well into my adulthood, my ministry, my family, and my relationships. I know now that when Jesus had the pianist pick "Just As I Am," the day I gave my heart to Him, it was more than a song. It was a prophetic word over my identity.

I KNOW NOW THAT WHEN JESUS HAD THE PIANIST PICK "JUST AS I AM," THE DAY I GAVE MY HEART TO HIM, IT WAS MORE THAN A SONG. IT WAS A PROPHETIC WORD OVER MY IDENTITY.

I had learned to hide the parts of myself I thought others might reject, and we can't be fully loved unless we're fully known, so it was self-sabotaging. I could preach circles about our value, identity, and worth. I'm one of the most confident people I know, but for the sake of authenticity, sometimes, we preach the messages we WANT to believe. As confident as I was on the outside, there was this small, nagging inner critic deeply rooted in rejection and constantly seeking approval from wherever I could get it. I'm glad the invention of social media didn't come until I was already an adult. I can't imagine what a train wreck that would have been.

I also want to clarify that in no way do I view my life through a lens of victimhood and I want to be clear about that. I've made costly mistakes in my lifetime too. I've learned to forgive things I never received an apology for and to extend the same grace that I've received. But sometimes we have to recognize that the lies we believe have much deeper roots than we can see on the surface. Sometimes, the things we think we've let go of haven't really let go of us. We've left Egypt, but Egypt still hangs out in our mindsets. Especially when it starts showing up in patterns over a long period of time, it may be an area where we need some healing and deliverance and counseling and quite literally a new mind.

This father wound rooted in rejection had me wasting actual years of my life trying to find acceptance and love in places and people I would *never* find it. It had me chasing belonging and saying yes to things I didn't really feel peace about. It had me feeling unworthy to sit around tables I knew I was called to. It had me chasing attention and value around like a stray dog, not realizing I was already royalty through adoption and sonship.

As an adult in full-time vocational ministry, it had me attaching my value to ministry assignments, getting my worthiness from the accolades of man instead of the voice of the Father alone. And when you live in that type of bondage, rejection feels fatal. I used to feel the constant need to defend my image and protect people's perceptions of me to avoid ever being rejected or unloved. My masks got thicker and thicker. I became a performer who learned not to disappoint anybody. It's hard to truly please God when you're living to please people, especially if you're in a culture that celebrates performance as a value.

As a pioneer/revivalist/reformer, you will often be met with the very resistance you constantly dread. I would be unable to sleep at night, lying awake thinking of ways I could be rejected for something God had me share. Funny how God can use what tried to destroy you to deliver you from bondage and actually propel you forward into your kingdom assignment. The same jealousy that threw Joseph into a pit and locked him in a prison led to the palace where his gifts would be used to save his people. Gifts are never about building up our brand. They're about serving the body. The rejection that tried to take me out, God is now using to set captives free. He's turned it around full circle. Your pain will become the platform His name is praised on.

YOUR PAIN WILL BECOME THE PLATFORM HIS NAME IS PRAISED ON.

I walked through a season of such intense rejection it actually was a tool God used to fully deliver me from rejection. It was so insane and ridiculous and unrelentingly painful and untrue to the character and fruit of my life, it would have taken more faith to actually believe it. I finally saw the spirit of rejection for what it really was. A tool driving me to the full acceptance of the Father. I realized we empower strongholds by coming into agreement with them. Break the curse of rejection so God can use you to break it off others! Nobody was more rejected than Jesus. His rejection was the ultimate sacrifice for our full acceptance. There is no opinion man can have that can erase what was finished on the cross. Man can cancel, betray, lie, attack, accuse, etc., but the Father is unmoved in His affection for you. He calls you UNCANCELED. Your response to rejection can actually cause you to level up.

If you were raised up in very performance-driven ministry models, then you probably know all too well that the problem with that is that the church wasn't made to operate like the systems and structures of this world. Our kingdom is not of this world. Yet when we adopt our values from culture instead of God's design for apostolic houses. People are often just a means to an end, a cog in the ministry wheel.

We'd never say that. It's mean. But the fruit sometimes proves it to be true. God's economy does not function like that. He will never ask you to sacrifice your health, your family, or the purity of what He has entrusted you to steward on the altar of performance and ladder-climbing. (Unless He's called you to be an *actual* performer, and in that case, be the best performer for Jesus you can be.)

I walked through a season of ministry several years ago when looking back now, I should have put myself in a time-out. I needed time to heal. Instead, my gifts propelled me right back into a season of vast promotion that I was not ready for. I was still attaching my worth to my work for the kingdom. A person who struggles with rejection will *really* struggle with sitting still in a season of refinement and correction. A word of caution: jumping off the Potter's wheel too soon and into promotion too early leads to an immature ministry mindset. It's dangerous, and the people who put you there are not loving you well. They may think they're helping, but they're setting you up to fail. I thank God for the people who told me to sit down because they cared more about the health of my soul than my performance and image.

A WORD OF CAUTION: JUMPING OFF THE POTTER'S WHEEL TOO SOON AND INTO PROMOTION TOO EARLY LEADS TO AN IMMATURE MINISTRY MINDSET.

Every church should have fathers and mothers on their team who just go around and make sure everyone is being loved well, connected in community, and emotionally healthy. We shouldn't shame people who need help. We all need help sometimes. Sabbaticals wouldn't be an emergency if rest were a required rhythm. Sometimes, we use our assignments and titles to hide our shame and inadequacy. A title and a platform will not deliver you from a spirit of rejection. It will only magnify it.

Titles and platforms also won't heal the failures of your past. It will only magnify the shame of it. I've used positions to mask shame. It only makes you feel like a hypocrite. Until you let Jesus heal you, nothing will make it better. Looking to anything other than Jesus to be the healer of your brokenness is futile. He is the only One who can affirm your value. The enemy is never intimidated by our public life or threatened by our titles. But he will struggle to pull down a saint who still looks like Jesus when nobody else is watching. He will struggle with a saint who has no shame left to hold onto. When the enemy tries to use shame to manipulate you into forfeiting your future, just let him know he's got the wrong address. Shame doesn't live here anymore. It's all been forwarded to Jesus. Shame is no longer your identity. Your talent, assignments, gifts, and titles are no longer your identity either. God alone defines you, and He calls you beloved.

Over the years, we saw miracles. We saw communities changed by the power of God. We saw families transformed. Marriages restored. The church revitalized. Health. Growth. Increase. Souls saved, baptized, and equipped in their unique callings. We saw God do things people said couldn't be done. Jesus did it. Our influence expanded. The testimony of what Jesus was doing spread. Powerful momentum and life were happening. And unknowingly, my value system was getting more tangled around all of it. If your identity isn't in Christ, friends, when the platform is removed or assignments end, you won't remember that the calling remains, and you're still standing on everything that matters.

Rejection builds you up, burns you out, and tears you down. It says, "Keep going! Push harder! Do more! You're accepted!" followed by, "Fight to stay accepted, and hide when you're in pain," followed by, "You're used up trash." Rinse, recycle, and repeat forever until you get freedom and new mindsets rooted in sonship. I've been beautifully set free from rejection and performance-driven ministry mindsets. I've learned how to stay free. His love can break cycles of rejection and striving. You can be free and stay free from the poison of rejection. He speaks a better declaration over you.

God opens doors, and God closes them. Our participation is in the stewardship of the open door. Poor stewardship of our soul will eventually cause us to implode from the inside out. It's funny how fast all those balls we juggle for people's approval can turn into giant crushing boulders. His yoke is easy, and His burden is light. When we start operating for love instead of from it, we take on burdens we aren't capable of carrying, and those burdens become our tomb.

GOD OPENS DOORS, AND GOD CLOSES THEM. OUR PARTICIPATION IS IN THE STEWARDSHIP OF THE OPEN DOOR.

We can blame others for putting those burdens on us, call out specific things *they* did wrong, and get nothing from it but a cup of bitterness and division in the body of Christ, or we can take personal responsibility for our own actions and grow. God favors humility. It's always the way through a mess. It doesn't matter how toxic or healthy the environment around you is, you *always* have a choice before you to steward the environment *inside* of you.

If you need to heal or get your heart right, pausing for a season is always a better option than cleaning up the mess from bulldozing over red flags. Seasons of rest always have an expiration. The Lord will use those seasons to unyoke you from lies you've believed and from the assignments and people He never ordained for you. He will use those seasons to lead you to the land He's promised, and He'll seat you at a table He built for you with His own hands. The healing and recompense coming to you is going to be beautiful.

At one time in my life, a mentor saw some of those red flags and gave me a gentle and loving pastoral warning to be careful and slow down because it looked like I couldn't keep up with the pace of my life. But I felt like the more I said yes to things, the more productive I was being for the kingdom—the greater the chasm between me and shame. The less I would be that little girl climbing a broken ladder. I'd finally belong at the table. Beloved, you belonged at the table before there was a table. He makes us worthy, and He doesn't use and abuse His children on altars of performance.

I hope you catch my heart in sharing this and know that I am not low-key trying to prop up my ego with this statement. But, if you're like me and have a lot of different gifts operating on your life, you're probably the person people trust to do a lot of things well. Toss in some performance-based ministry mindsets, and you're probably carrying a lot more than you should be.

Usually, I'm not overseeing one thing at a time. More often than not, I'm given responsibility over dozens of things at a time. You could view it from a lens of God rewarding faithfulness—which is true. But sometimes, our need for approval says yes to things our capacity and character can't carry for the long haul. We only have grace for the things God has actually called us to. Nothing is heavier than trying to operate outside of your grace.

At one time in my life, I was running a local newspaper office, writing, and reporting the county news. Directing the chamber of commerce. Pastoring a church full-time and wearing a lot of hats inside that hat. Leading worship. Planning outreaches. Traveling. Speaking. Homeschooling three little boys. And I was a wife and a friend who said yes to everything.

I kept blazing those pioneering trails, and my friend was absolutely right. I couldn't keep up with the pace of my life. I had no more capacity to care for my soul at the level it needed. It was open season, and there was a big target on my back. I was exposed, depleted, and burned out. The enemy doesn't always take us out with blatant compromise. Sometimes premature success is a time-bomb all on its own. Word to the wise: surround yourself with people who tell you what you *need* to hear, not just what you *want* to hear. Jesus doesn't burn us out to make Himself famous. He is famous all by Himself. He doesn't need us to make Him anything. He's always everything. Sometimes, the Lord breaks our ladders to reveal His nature. Other times, He breaks them to rescue us from ourselves.

WORD TO THE WISE: SURROUND YOURSELF WITH PEOPLE WHO TELL YOU WHAT YOU NEED TO HEAR, NOT JUST WHAT YOU WANT TO HEAR.

You can sprint at a wild pace, but try enduring a marathon at that same speed. Not possible. The energy can only last a very short distance. My husband and sons bought me a DNA test a few years ago for my birthday, and I found out I have the same genetic variant found in the DNA of elite power athletes. It's this common link between professional sprinters, throwers, and jumpers.

Now, if you *know* me, that's probably funny because the only time I'm going to be running fast is if I'm being chased by a bear. I don't have to be the fastest in that scenario; I just can't be the slowest. My point is this: ministry is not a sprint. It's a marathon. It requires longevity. What's the point of getting somewhere fast if you're uprooted by the warfare when you get there? You can't go the distance and take your spiritual health lightly.

Hosea's prophecy reminds me of myself:

> "Therefore, behold, I will allure her, and bring her into the wilderness, and speak tenderly to her. And there I will give her her vineyards and make the Valley of Achor a door of hope. And there she shall answer as in the days of her youth, as at the time when she came out of the land of Egypt.
>
> "And in that day, declares the LORD, you will call me 'My Husband,' and no longer will you call me 'My Baal.' For I will remove the names of the Baals from her mouth, and they shall be remembered by name no more." —Hosea 2:14-17 (ESV)

God set me free in a wilderness. He kept me warm by the fire He built with my little broken ladder. He turned my valley of trouble into a door of hope. Doors swing both ways. Hope for me. Hope for you. Living under that yoke of striving is weary. If you're reading this book, I'm guessing you've been feeling a pull into something more. Something different. You're frustrated by the long season of silence, longing for change but not even knowing what that looks like, expecting a door to open, but it hasn't. I just want to speak encouragement to your soul. This wilderness isn't punishment. It's preparing you for the promise. It's preparing you for longevity.

Maybe you recognize areas where you're doing stuff for validation. You are starting to see places where you've compromised purity and replaced it with consumer Christianity. Or maybe you haven't seen it all. This is the moment when scales are falling off your eyes, and God is revealing areas He wants to transform. One thing is for certain. Anything we try to build with our own hands, we have to maintain with our own hands.

Climbing ladders of self-promotion is not your portion. I think, on some level, we've all experienced some form of rejection or another. We all have a basic human need to be validated. To belong. To matter. But when we start filling that need with counterfeit significance, platform building, ladder climbing, people pleasing, name dropping, and blasting all of our activity on social media to appear impressive... we've started building our own lowercase "k" kingdoms.

THE HEAVENLY REALITY IS YOU WERE LOVED BEFORE YOU EVER DID ANYTHING WORTHY OF IT. READ THAT AGAIN. LET IT SINK IN.

The only problem with attaching our identity to an assignment or a person's opinion is that when assignments and opinions change, we're left wondering who we are. The heavenly reality is you were loved before you ever did anything worthy of it. Read that again. Let it sink in. Failure isn't final, and rejection isn't fatal. The church is a place to lay down our lives and pick up our crosses; it was never meant to be the place we build personal platforms or prop our identities on.

The thief on the cross entered the same paradise Jesus did before He ever had an opportunity to prove how impressive He could be. The only name we should be dropping is the name of Jesus. Our clout may impress man, but it does not impress heaven. All of the things we build unto ourselves will burn up one day, and the only thing that will remain is what we build for Him.

There's a quote I love by Bill Johnson: "If you don't live for the praise of man, you won't die from their criticism." The favor and approval of man are fickle. Nobody understands like Jesus does how fickle the crowd can be. Some plotting. Some praising. If you're looking for approval, don't look to the crowd. It's always a mix of both. Look no further than Jesus. His opinions of you are rooted in HIS goodness (not your performance) and have much more enduring qualities.

What if the broken ladder is a gift? What if that rejection was a rescue plan from a life of striving for significance? What if the stripping away is actually taking you down to the very foundation of just being loved by Him? Friend, don't attach your identity to your assignment. You're more than what your hands can build. You're more than what your gifts can do. If you don't have an identity deeply rooted in sonship, you will look to things and people to give you what only Jesus can.

You'll get sucked into the whirlpool of platform worship, flexing, clout, and striving. Your gifting and anointing make space for you at the table. You don't need to self-promote. You don't need to announce your worth to a room you're called to be in. Your Father actually delights in introducing you to that room.

My adopted dad passed away unexpectedly in 2017 as we were driving in from out of state to attend my grandma's funeral. We were a few hours away from getting one of the best hugs ever when I got a call that my dad suffered a heart attack and died instantly. We pulled the car off the highway and told our children. We cried, worshiped, prayed, and pushed on toward home by the grace of God. My mom held my grandmother as she took her last breath and, a few days later, held my dad as he took his.

There was so much to properly grieve, but I wouldn't even give myself space for it because I had to maintain this image of having my life all together. The times I did grieve publicly felt like ministry too. I was modeling how to worship through suffering. For some reason, needing ministry and comfort from the church felt like an opportunity to be rejected because there was this deep lie from the beginning that I had to do more than everyone else to be worthy. Pride will always keep the help you need at arm's length. I didn't want to jeopardize my image with vulnerability. But vulnerability is what connects us in authentic community. I ended up burying my grandma and then preaching at my dad's funeral the following week while trying to comfort our children and pastoring like my world hadn't just turned upside down.

One of the things I loved most about my adopted dad was how he always announced me to a room. From some of my earliest memories, he was so proud to show me off. He'd compliment my beauty. He'd praise my accomplishments. But mostly, he was always shouting about my identity as his daughter: "There's my baby girl!" Fathers and mothers, if you want to raise healthy sons and daughters who go the distance, celebrate who they are *more* than what they produce for the institution. It was the Lord's grace having him as a dad and a true prophetic picture of how we're adopted and fully accepted sons and daughters.

The Lord wants to break the orphan spirit in the church. The comparison and self-promotion. The heart motivated by results and the esteem of man. The constant fear and paranoia of being overlooked. The self-isolation and hiding. That place of always feeling victimized. The performance mindset that keeps you stuck in cycles of constantly trying to prove your worthiness. God completely can set you free. He calls you beloved. So just be loved.

You don't need to be noticed, recognized, discovered, or favored by man because in the right season, your Father will position you exactly where He's called you to be. I no longer feel a need to explain my anointing to people or peacock my uniqueness around like some kind of badge of honor to my Christlikeness.

My Father delights in revealing who I am to others, and what He values most isn't my credentials or the title glued to my door; it's my identity as His child. Sonship is the most important ship of all the "ships." It is foundational. You're more than your leadership. You're more than your friendships. You're more than who you're standing next to. You're more than a tool in God's belt He only pulls out to use. We are loved. We aren't a means to an end or a cog in a wheel, keeping the ministry machine progressing onward and upward. We aren't an asset to His kingdom. He calls us friends, co-heirs, adopted sons and daughters, priests, saints, beloved. Everything about the language He speaks is in the context of family.

> **YOU'RE MORE THAN WHO YOU'RE STANDING NEXT TO. YOU'RE MORE THAN A TOOL IN GOD'S BELT HE ONLY PULLS OUT TO USE.**

To avoid the vulnerability of intimacy, we've changed the language to make the church sound more like a corporation than a bride. Maybe it's because we can control and dispose of employees more easily if we don't call them sons. Let's use the Father's language. Everything the Father does is in the context of family. He is entirely relational. He isn't a CEO. We aren't employees. Even our gifts are meant to pull us into a closer relationship with Him. It's scary how well we can use gifts without intimacy.

Often, it would be less messy just doing it all by Himself, as every parent knows, but life without you was never something He wanted. I think God's heart is eager and earnest for His beloved to stop striving and competing for a seat at His table, building impressive platforms when all He wanted was an altar and our hearts. We aren't sons of the slave women. There is work to be done, and the Father delights in seeing the work begin, but if we say no, it will still get done because the church was never about us and our titles and talents. It was always His.

The church didn't stop when the apostles were martyred. It doesn't stop when we are promoted into a wilderness of obscurity. It doesn't stop when houses split and leaders fall. It doesn't stop when the gates of hell rise up against her. It doesn't stop when people leave ugly. Pandemics can't stop her. Your failures can't stop her. Our egos can't stop her. Accusation can't stop her. The church never stops because Christ is the head. So why are we striving so hard to hold everything together like it depends on us?

Let me say it again: We are working *from* love. Never for it. *From* identity. Never for it. Don't confuse your do with His done. He said, "It is finished," so we'd know for certain we earn nothing in the exchange. Your gifts, anointing, assignment, and calling are NOT platforms you build on, trophies you earn, or ladders you climb. You have an assignment, but you ARE a loved child—born of promise with nothing to prove, just like the apostle Paul said:

> And you did not receive the "spirit of religious duty" leading you back into the fear of never being good enough. But you have received the "Spirit of full acceptance," enfolding you into the family of God.
> —Romans 8:15 (TPT)

> **PIONEER PRAYER:**
> *Jesus, I invite You to break my ladders.—each and every one. Uproot every bit of striving, performance, and platform worship from my life. I lay down my reputation and pick up Your cross. Expose the hidden places of self-promotion. Show me the areas I've been working for love and identity instead of from it. Thank You that I have an assignment, but more than that, thank You that I am loved. Amen.*

Pioneer Prompt:

You won't be free to pioneer if you're still yoked to the approval of man. Get in a quiet space with God. Draw a ladder, and on each step, ask the Lord to reveal any areas where you've been attaching your value and identity to assignments, people, titles, and positions. Beside each step, write what the Lord is speaking over your identity in that area of struggle. Allow His love to dismantle the ladder of striving.

_____

_____

_____

_____

_____

_____

_____

_____

_____

_____

_____

_____

CHAPTER 4

The Résumé

Celebrating is a core value in our family. We celebrate everything. I believe whatever you celebrate, you get more of. We celebrate Jewish feasts and holidays. (We're not Jewish, but we know the significance of going to the parties Jesus would have attended.) We celebrate many made-up days, too, like "Fall Hunt," where we surprise each other with a gift and hunt for it on Thanksgiving Day to show our gratitude.

We celebrate weekly Sabbath rest, Shabbat dinners, and praying blessings over our sons. We celebrate birthdays, countdowns to birthdays, spiritual birthdays, and even birthdays of family and pets who have passed away. My middle son, David, is on my party planning committee. We like to plan birthday scavenger hunts together. When our boys turn thirteen, we celebrate with a rite of passage for them as they step into the next season toward manhood. Basically, my house always has leftover, half-deflated balloons randomly lying around everywhere.

This value for celebration has definitely been passed on to our sons because now they make up their own reasons to celebrate and show honor. We have an annual Christmas tree hunt and celebrate finding the perfect tree with hot cocoa and classic Christmas movies. Then, at the end of every year, we take communion and fill a jar with memories of God's faithfulness throughout the year while we worship and let God speak a word into the coming year. We open previous years' jars and read out loud the miracles, provisions, surprises, blessings, and moments of God's goodness that we've recorded. These traditions and celebrations are sacred to us.

Through no desire or will of my own, I've somehow become the balloon lady. If there's an event of any kind, it's, "Rhea, can you make a balloon arch for the photo booth?"

"Sure thing!"

I have no idea. It's like the balloon favor of God is resting on my life. I even get random balloon requests from people I don't know. I think it's just God's way of helping me get rid of all the hot air. Ha-ha! Or maybe a reminder that we are created to celebrate.

You get to set the atmosphere you allow into your home. We believe celebration and honor are values in the kingdom that open the door for powerful moves of God. We've seen the fruit of that. We've also seen the fruit of the times it's been World War III chaos in our home, and the fruit is not as delightful. Every day, we unknowingly plant hundreds of tiny seeds that are going to hit the soil. Hopefully, they produce a harvest that's good. It might not even be a harvest we see, but whether we see it or not, sow with the end in mind.

> **EVERY DAY, WE UNKNOWINGLY PLANT HUNDREDS OF TINY SEEDS THAT HOPEFULLY PRODUCE A HARVEST THAT'S GOOD... BUT WHETHER WE SEE IT OR NOT, SOW WITH THE END IN MIND.**

We should also love celebrating the victories of others. I am emotionally invested in seeing people honored. I've watched *The Lord of the Rings: The Return of the King* a zillion times and still cry when (spoiler alert—if you've been living under a rock) the hobbits are honored at the movie's end. The king says, "My friends, you bow to no one," and then everyone in the kingdom bows to *them*, including the king.[5] Honor moves me. I think it moves the Father too.

Your success doesn't threaten me because if I do life with you, I've probably prayed for it. I'm not hoping you fail. I'm not hoping my worst enemies fail. I pray victory and favor over the people who have slandered, attacked, accused, lied, gossiped about, spiritually abused, and rejected me. Because we're a whole *body*, your victory is mine, mine is yours, and we rise together. If you're winning, the enemy is losing. You win. I win. It's like Jesus said in Mark 9:40 (author paraphrase), "If they're not against us, they're for us." When the heart button was introduced on Facebook, I thrived: "You get a heart. You get a heart. Everyone gets a heart!" Why even keep the like button?

---

5 *The Lord of the Rings: The Return of the King*, directed by Peter Jackson (2003; New York, NY: New Line Cinemas).

I say ALL that, so that you really hear my heart and this next part doesn't sound like I'm the Grinch who stole your Christmas. Exhortation is not fluffy, unicorn, kitten, rainbow sparkles. It's actually a very misunderstood gift—meant *not* to just build you up. Obviously, that's the goal of all prophetic gifts: to edify, exhort, equip, and comfort. But it also is a gift that brings the loving correction of the Lord and urges hearts back into alignment with the Father:

> Examine your motives to make sure you're not showing off when you do your good deeds, only to be admired by others; otherwise, you will lose the reward of your heavenly Father. So when you give to the poor, don't announce it and make a show of it just to be seen by people, like the hypocrites in the streets and in the marketplace. They've already received their reward! But when you demonstrate generosity, do it with pure motives and without drawing attention to yourself. Give secretly and your Father, who sees all you do, will reward you openly.
> —Matthew 6:1-4 (TPT)

Every time we announce our moves with the hidden motive of receiving public validation, we run the risk of trading eternal rewards for temporary human accolades. It's like it says in Proverbs 27:2 (TPT): "Let someone else honor you for your accomplishments, for self-praise is never appropriate." There are a lot of rewards floating around on social media, and that's where they're going to stay. God isn't trying to suck the fun out of our celebration and creativity. He just wants to purify it. He's after our motives.

In addition to co-pastoring our house church, worship leading, creative directing, and wearing a bunch of other hats in this season, I am also a graphic designer for a publishing company and the social media director of our church. I've overcome a lot of warfare in this area, so there's some authority on what I want to speak into next. I don't care how many followers you have or who likes your posts, none of them are worth your soul. Not one of those voices should be replacing the voice of your Father. Don't sell your birthright for a bowl of soup.

Don't spend your days building your public image and missing Jesus. If you don't guard your heart and have designated times when the phone stays off, those likes, comments, and followers can cause you to become addicted to a false sense of validation. It can cause you to even trade eternal rewards for temporary ones. And if you don't set boundaries and be present in *reality*, they will also disconnect you from the people and things that truly matter.

There are going to be a lot of rewards given out in heaven to unknown people with small followings. These individuals may not have enough clout in the realms of human measurements of value to get a little blue verified check by their Instagram, but they have A LOT of clout in heaven. They do all their works for an audience of One—and He is fully captivated.

THERE ARE GOING TO BE A LOT OF REWARDS GIVEN OUT IN HEAVEN TO UNKNOWN PEOPLE WITH SMALL FOLLOWINGS. THEY DO ALL THEIR WORKS FOR AN AUDIENCE OF ONE—AND HE IS FULLY CAPTIVATED.

Paul's résumé, in the moments he had to defend his apostleship, looked nothing like those we craft today. In 2 Corinthians 11:22 (TPT), Paul sarcastically called out the "super-apostles" who were preaching a different gospel than the one they had received and were leading people into deception. He mockingly stated he was acting like a fool to boast about his accomplishments as others did, and basically in verses 23-33, he said, "Humor me while I go through the list of my qualifications:

> "I've worked harder, been put in prison more than anyone else, and whipped a countless number of times. Five different times, the Jewish leaders gave me thirty-nine lashes. Three times, I was beaten with rods. Once, I was stoned. Three times, I was shipwrecked. Once, I spent a whole night and day adrift at sea. I've embarked on long, perilous journeys. I've had to be lowered in a basket through the window of a city wall to escape with my life as I've faced dangers from robbers, false believers, my own people, and Gentiles. I've encountered danger in the deserts and cities and on the seas. I've been hungry, thirsty, tired, and homeless. I've shivered in the cold without enough clothes to keep me warm. Oh, and besides that, I have the daily burden of caring for all these churches."

If I were Paul, that would have been an excellent place to insert a mic drop and just walk out of the room. Paul was modeling a profound apostolic picture for the church to grasp. He understood the power of preaching his weakness. There are so many hidden agendas calling the shots sometimes, that we don't even recognize what's pure anymore. In performance-driven cultures, our brains are always formulating, calculating, and strategizing. Even simple things like prioritizing family are calculated: "This is how successful people operate, so I'm going follow that formula," or "This is how the Spirit moved last time, so I'm gonna follow that formula." It makes those close to you question your sincerity when everything becomes a formula to follow.

Never in a million years, would most of us want to put our issues on blast like Paul did: "If I must boast, I would rather boast about the things that show how weak I am" (2 Corinthians 11:30, NLT). If we had Paul's qualifications and experiences, most of our social media would look like the following. (Indulge me in some silly banter for a moment.)

- » Raised this kid from the dead today. It was wild. Dude fell out a window. Moral of the story: Don't fall asleep in the middle of my sermons. Glad I was there to help. (Posts group selfie with resurrected child.)
- » Check out this tent I made today. Not perfect, but I did my best. (Posts selfie smiling in front of the most perfect tent ever made.)
- » Got to share the gospel with King Agrippa today. #Humbled (Posts photo outside the palace.)
- » Had a great time meeting Ananias. It really opened my eyes. #ICanSeeAgain #Grateful
- » Wrote another epistle. My hands are sore, but it was worth it. All glory to Jesus. Hope you're all having a great day. (Posts selfie from prison cell.)

» Planted my seventh church today. Work hard. Play hard. #AllGloryToGod (Posts selfie playing golf with all the leaders.)

Ha-ha! All in good fun. We can laugh at ourselves still, right? If it stings or offends you, it's not condemnation. I propose it may be a place God is inviting you into a deep revelation of His freedom. Paul didn't sign his letters "Dr. Paul" or "Apostle, Pastor, Teacher, Tent Maker, Missionary Paul." He was just "Paul." Social media is such a powerful tool, but sometimes, we can worship tools if we're running to them for validation before letting Jesus speak into our identity and sift our motives.

Sometimes, our self-promotion actually reeks of insecurity. It doesn't actually accomplish what we hope it will. It only serves to reveal an area of our lives where we're still living like orphans, begging for scraps at the table: *I don't feel inherent value from the kingdom I was adopted into, so I need YOU to define that for me.* Orphans say yes to things they should say no to.

I've had to go through deep, gut-wrenching cleansing to get to a place where I can even have this conversation without crawling out of my skin. If I were reading this book to myself several years ago, I'd be like: *Well, that's not my struggle. I'm not proud. I'm not seeking praise. I just want to give God glory.* Denial ain't just a river in Egypt, y'all. God can't heal what we won't get honest about.

GOD CAN'T HEAL WHAT WE WON'T GET HONEST ABOUT.

I remember one particular ministry season when we experienced tremendous fruitfulness. It was like fruit was popping up where we hadn't even sown a harvest. I was publicly celebrating every bit of it. I eventually just kept a helium tank in my office in case I needed to blow up some balloons at any moment. I'm pretty sure most of my ministry budget was spent on cupcakes, balloons, and confetti. #AllGloryToJesus

We had hundreds upon hundreds of unbelievable ministry victories. Was our enthusiasm motivated by seeing the family of God expand—100 percent, yes! Do we know whom the glory goes to? Absolutely. Was I feeling excited for people to see how successful our ministry was? Also yes. Was I getting tons of personal validation from the likes and comments section? Yep. Maybe you're too holy to relate to that, but remember what I said at the beginning of the book? I'm committed to appropriate vulnerability. I think if we're honest with ourselves, a lot of things we share publicly aren't as necessary as we think they are. Our posts may actually be revealing areas we lack identity.

You probably have some stories too, killing yourself for just a few bread crumbs of approval when you could be feasting at the table Jesus already prepared for you. I mastered the art of catching the best possible angle of everything. I would get privately annoyed if someone posted a picture that made a room look empty. Validation can feel like money in the bank of our souls. But those small deposits come with a hefty interest rate. I wonder what other occupation exchanges purity for some form of compensation. Oh, right—prostitution.

The Pharisees loved flattery. Sincere compliments are encouraging, but compliments with hidden agendas are actually a form of manipulation, which is witchcraft. Usually, people who operate in this spirit talk out of both sides of their mouths—flattery on one side and division on the other. The Pharisees loved seats of honor, attaboys, titles, and their own image of self-importance. It was all about who you know and where you sit at the table. Sound familiar? God isn't sorry when our pride is wounded. He would rather it be dead.

What did Jesus have to say about it?

> "They love to sit at the head table at church dinners, basking in the most prominent positions, preening in the radiance of public flattery, receiving honorary degrees, and getting called 'Doctor' or 'Reverend.' . . . Do you want to stand out? Then step down. Be a servant. If you puff yourself up, you'll get the wind knocked out of you. But if you're content to simply be yourself, your life will count for plenty." —Matthew 23:4-7 and 11-12 (MSG)

God has had to take more than a few chips off my shoulders. He is great at taking us down a peg or two when we become victims of our own smugness. He loves us too much to allow us to stay stuck in self-delusion. True humility recognizes who we are without Jesus AND embraces who we are because of Him. We know *some* things, but we don't know *all* things. In Christ, we have immense value, and believing anything less is religious garbage. The anointing doesn't increase our value or make us better than others. Believing it does will be our undoing.

Humility is not being a doormat. It's not passivity. It's not your proximity to the platform. It's not shrinking back. It's not watering down your oil to make others more comfortable. It's not acting like you're not good enough. The most humble posture is walking in the abundant life Jesus promised us in John 10:10.

Jesus exposed the hypocrisy of the religious leaders:

> "You're hopeless, you Pharisees! Frauds! You love sitting at the head table at church dinners, love preening yourselves in the radiance of public flattery. Frauds! You're just like unmarked graves: People walk over that nice, grassy surface, never suspecting the rot and corruption that is six feet under."
> —Luke 11:43-44 (MSG)

The Pharisees customarily were prohibited from touching dead things. It was considered defilement. Unclean. But they covered their true dead condition with a substance that had the appearance of life. Some things that seem attractive and full of life are actually a trap and full of death. Sometimes, we care about the *appearance* of life more than what's actually going on in our hearts. We all disapprove of the Pharisees until Jesus points out the ways we are one. Professional Christianity is not our portion.

We need to make our daily prayer, "Jesus, reveal the Pharisee in me." Clean up all the hypocrisy. The conversations are different when we operate from sonship. We stop pointing people to our image of self-importance and start pointing them to Jesus. If our ministries only lead people to us, we've failed. When we yoke our value to our external success instead of Jesus, we get sucked into a continual cycle of rejection, shame, and performance. Satan was the first "orphan" and he has had thousands of years to perfect the skill of using rejection to make you behave like one too. It's time to break out of this cycle. The weak parts of our story and even rejection can connect people to the heart of the Father more than our pretend holiness ever could. It's not glorifying our sin and rebellion or putting on false humility. Receiving a compliment well isn't going to steal God's glory. We're not that powerful.

False humility is true pride. It's bondage. It's the opposite of humility. Every accusing voice was silenced when the first hammer stroke hit the first nail. Thinking less of yourself is vastly different from thinking of yourself less. It's okay to be proud of the fruit of your life. Humility doesn't put confidence in the flesh but in Christ. I know who I am without Jesus, and knowing that protects my heart. I know who I am capable of being without His presence. I depend on Him and put no more confidence in my flesh.

THE ENEMY LOVES IT WHEN WE STOP SHARING TESTIMONIES BECAUSE THOSE STORIES ARE THE BIRTHPLACES OF BREAKTHROUGH FOR SOMEONE ELSE. IT'S BLOCKED WORSHIP WHEN WE HOLD HIS GOODNESS CAPTIVE.

Orphans perform for love and never feel like what they bring is enough. Have you ever used a translator app, and somehow, it has you saying things all wonky from your original intent? That's what's happened here. Somewhere along the way, we thought humility meant not having any confidence when the most humble thing we could do is have confidence rightly placed in Jesus. It's not about denying your worthiness. It's about recognizing the *Source* of it. The devil would hate for us to realize the weapon that is our testimony. I'm NOT saying shut praise down because of fear of losing a reward or looking arrogant. People will always misunderstand you. Stay obedient. The enemy loves it when we stop sharing testimonies because those stories are the birthplaces of breakthrough for someone else. It's blocked worship when we hold His goodness captive.

The Lord's résumé is flawless, and we should shout it from the rooftops. Ours is not, and that's okay to shout from the rooftops too! I have literal libraries of miracles just in my own life. I ride those waves regularly and catch new ones. I will obnoxiously exalt the Lord until I die. When we value what God does, it builds atmospheres of hope in the retelling of those stories. Our worthiness comes from the Father's approval. A.W. Tozer said, "The most portentous fact about any man is not what he at a given time may say or do, but what he in his deep heart conceives God to be like." Before Jesus' earthly ministry began, The Father looked at Him and said, "This is my Beloved Son, with whom I am well pleased." That is the nature of our Father. He loves us before we do anything to deserve it.

We should be more concerned with God getting glory than fearful someone might misjudge our motives. Steward your motives well, and God will trust you with more. We forfeit a lot of rewards because our motivations are wrong. Carrying orphan mindsets will influence our motives and negatively impact our ministries. We have divided adulterous hearts co-loving our Husband Jesus and also craving the esteem of men. I think Jesus gave a very kingdom solution to all of us celebrators who love to blast what God is doing from the rooftops—as well as all of us who are breaking out of cycles of rejection. In Luke 10:17 (NLT), when the seventy-two disciples returned from a ministry assignment Jesus had sent them on, they were in full celebration mode: "Demons obey us when we use your name!" That's an exciting revelation they didn't have twenty-four hours before.

It's interesting that Jesus didn't rebuke them for what sort of seems like an inflated sense of importance. Instead, in verse 18 (NLT), He affirmed them by saying, "I saw Satan fall from heaven like lightning." Then, He affirmed them again by revealing even MORE of their authority: "Look, I have given you authority over all the power of the enemy, and you can walk among snakes and scorpions and crush them. Nothing will injure you" (verse 19, NLT).

Finally, though, in Luke 10:20 (NLT), He brought it back to the heart of the matter as He often did: "But don't rejoice because evil spirits obey you; rejoice because your names are registered in heaven." And there it is. Motives matter most to Jesus. A heart postured to be searched by the Lord can get more accomplished for the kingdom than all the strategy meetings on how to get people to walk through a church door.

Allowing the Holy Spirit to sift my motives has become a daily habit because I want to go the distance. I ask myself, *Why am I really sharing this?* I'm not afraid to ask those questions. I'm not afraid of what He'll find. My heart is an open book to Him. He is full of grace, and I'm beloved. I've had to say no to things that would make me look way better if I said yes. I've had to hide some huge victories because I didn't feel the Lord's approval for me to share them. I stopped casting all my pearls on a platform that trampled them. I stopped posting every ministry event. I've had to disappoint people's expectations and allow people to believe lies about me when a simple conversation could clear my name. I've had to rip up my résumé.

I took a year off social media. I fast from these platforms regularly, and I don't announce it because I don't owe the world an explanation for my obedience. This is how the Lord trained me to walk out my deliverance from a performance-based ministry mindset. How you walk out yours will be different, but to form new mindsets in any area you're struggling with, you HAVE to form new habits, and this is why:

> "The world offers only a craving for physical pleasure, a craving for everything we see, and pride in our achievements and possessions. These are not from the Father, but are from this world. And this world is fading away, along with everything that people crave. But anyone who does what pleases God will live forever. —1 John 2:16-17 (NLT)

We need the loving gaze of God, probing our motives and agendas deeply and burning us with a love that makes us holy.

Our motives get twisted when we're more focused on our brand than being branded by His presence. The Refiner's fire is a thousand times more sustainable than self-promotion. Motives are God territory (see Proverbs 16:2), but so many times, we focus our zeal for correction outward when it should be pointed inward. We're calling people out for their little specks all while blindly knocking everyone around us out with the giant plank sticking out of our own eyeball. The Bible says we don't see the full picture. Anything we think we know about someone is just a glimpse—at best. At worst, it's an accusation ministry disguised as a discernment ministry.

THE BIBLE SAYS WE DON'T SEE THE FULL PICTURE. ANYTHING WE THINK WE KNOW ABOUT SOMEONE IS JUST A GLIMPSE—AT BEST. AT WORST, IT'S AN ACCUSATION MINISTRY DISGUISED AS A DISCERNMENT MINISTRY.

All revelation is partial, so who can boast that they've cornered the market on wisdom? (See 1 Corinthians 13:9.) Being wise in our own eyes is futile. Early in my walk, I used to think my discernment was infallible. I'd burn bridges. Call people out. Not in a mean way—but a private, well-meaning, obnoxious kind of way. I've made wild assumptions and harsh accusations based on nothing. I've made messes on the road to maturity. I'm sure I'll make more. But we're not loving people well if we're also beating them with our gifts. God won't show me your hidden dirt, but He will daily open the curtains, let the light in, and show me my own.

Motives aren't about anyone else's heart but MY OWN heart laid open before the Lord. Nothing hidden. He sees every mistake we've ever made yet loves us as if He never saw any of it. He was the sacrifice that wiped the slate clean. Nothing we could do could make it any cleaner. Know your authority, but understand that it's *borrowed* authority. You didn't earn your gifts any more than you earned your salvation any more than you earned the authority you operate from. It's all free. It's all grace.

So don't be more impressed with outward manifestations of who you are in Christ than in your identity as a son or daughter. The only position that matters is where we stand before the Father. We relegate far too much authority to our titles, accomplishments, and alignments instead of to the power of the blood of Jesus operating in our lives.

Demons don't obey us because we scream at them, forcefully rebuke them, or read a bunch of books and learn a bunch of spiritual-sounding language. Growing in our gifts is great, but worshiping our gifts instead of the Giver is not wise. Demons have knowledge about Jesus too. They don't respect us based on whose image we prop ourselves up against or the esteem of men or how scary we sound shouting them down. Anytime we try to accomplish spiritual things through human effort and not through the authority of the blood, we've become the sons of Sceva, and this is what the demons said to them in Acts 19:15 (TPT): "I know about Jesus, and I recognize Paul, but who do you think you are?" Our ministry titles and the accolades we've received do not set captives free. It's always been Jesus. It's always going to be Jesus.

There is a hyper-focus on demonic activity that is getting out of control and causing massive deception and division in the body of Christ. You'd almost think there are more demons than angels. When we build our theology around deliverance instead of the *Deliverer*, things get wonky. The seven sons of Sceva learned this lesson. Who we know, the institutions we attend, or the titles before our names—none of that matters to the enemy. So much of this hyper-spirituality is rooted in wanting impressive résumés: "Look at me. Demons obey me! I'm special."

A SPIRIT-FILLED WHISPER WORKS JUST AS WELL AS SHOUTING AT HELL UNTIL YOUR VOICE IS RAW.

A Spirit-filled whisper works just as well as shouting at hell until your voice is raw. Our external posture doesn't intimidate hell. It's the One whose name brands our hearts. (See Matthew 8:16.) All the authority in the world will never be more impressive than the reality of being a child of God. It's a mystery not even angelic beings are privileged to. It is a grace reserved for us alone and never earned through human striving, and Paul makes that clear:

> Some are preaching out of jealousy and rivalry. But others preach about Christ with pure motives. They

preach because they love me, for they know I have been appointed to defend the Good News. Those others do not have pure motives as they preach about Christ. They preach with selfish ambition, not sincerely, intending to make my chains more painful to me. But that doesn't matter. Whether their motives are false or genuine, the message about Christ is being preached either way, so I rejoice. And I will continue to rejoice. —Philippians 1:15-18 (NLT)

Other people's motives are God's realm. We are not a better judge than Jesus (even though sometimes we act like we are). The ONLY person's heart you're called to steward is your own. That is a full-time assignment all by itself. Be careful not to stand on the sidelines in judgment toward those who are actually in the game.

We see many people with big titles being taken out prematurely by pride or bad behavior. The church is a big part of the problem when we fan-girl and fuel celebrity culture in the body of Christ, and we need to repent. Character alone will take your gifts and anointing the distance. However, we lift their giftedness sky high and then throw stones when their character isn't strong enough to hold under the weight of it. We very much are part of the problem. They're just people who deserve honor like everyone else. Many of them didn't seek fame. They were just faithfully trying to serve the church. WE propped them up.

Celebrity Christianity is also an incubator for failure, but influence isn't the problem. Nothing tests a heart like influence and success. It's also an incubator for the gospel to be multiplied and the kingdom expanded. The fate of a ministry doesn't rise or fall on influence but on *stewardship*. Where compromise is not involved, sometimes God is pruning to make space for more of what He values because there has been excellent stewardship. Are we able to judge that? I'd say no.

Don't be quick to mark a church or person as healthy based on popularity or their ability to meet all your emotional needs. The crowd is fickle, and popular isn't always healthy. Fruit that is judged over a long period of time paints a more accurate picture from close proximity and a filter of love. God wants us to have influence, and He measures it out based on His will and our stewardship of the small things. We weren't made to worship man, influence, or impressive résumés. We weren't made to get fat off the glory that belongs to God.

It's not only the fallen celebrity pastor at fault. It's the consumer-driven church that tried to elevate them to a position higher than God in the first place by craving entertainment more than being fathered and mothered and loved and corrected. God guarantees to bring everything hidden in darkness into the light—not just a warning to the people with the microphones but also to those hiding sin in the pews.

All exposure is to lead us into deeper realms of freedom and love. Some people's exposure happens on a much larger platform, but it is not because their sin is worse than others. God disciplines those He loves, so if anything, it reveals a God who loves them as people more than He loves their platform or our entertainment. Let's remember these are REAL people Jesus loves and not jump on the keyboard warrior phenomenon. We're all braver behind the screen of our phones, but biblical correction is served up best through loving relationship.

All of our sin eventually gets uncovered. That's the nature of sin. It promises pleasure without consequence. God loves us too much to allow our junk to stay hidden, so let's all just collectively drop our stones and lean into grace. The mercy we show others is the mercy we will receive. (See James 2:13.) When it comes to the downfall of "Celebrity" Christians, if we're looking for someone to blame, maybe we should look in the mirror. We *wanted* performance-driven ministry. We contributed to it with our time and resources. We even mimicked it and made it the gold standard. We shopped around for it like consumers at Costco. We left houses that were healthy to chase it.

God is declaring that the days of consumer Christianity are coming to an end, and here comes the return of kingdom-modeled ministries and Christ-modeled mindsets. Like heaven and earth colliding. Like the marriage of Acts 2 and Acts 13. Gathering and sending. Meals and miracles. God is more concerned with fruit than forms. The church is a people, so the forms should be as vast and endless, but some forms have style without substance. You can spend a lifetime there without ever really being known by anyone or having to commit to anything. We never find the thing we're longing for because it's formed in family, and we've spent a lifetime isolating ourselves from that level of vulnerability. Whatever your form, don't love it so much you start worshiping a style and miss Jesus.

WHEN A LEADER BURNS THEMSELVES OUT BECAUSE THE LIGHT SHINING ON THEM WAS MEANT FOR GOD, THE CROWD TURNS. ALWAYS.

When a leader burns themselves out because the light shining on them was meant for God, the crowd turns. Always. How fickle fame can be: "We don't care about you as a person; we just want to be entertained and fed." Spiritualized gossip is becoming a favorite pastime for the church. The horror of things you read from "believers" on social media reveals more about the critic than it ever did about the person who was exposed. More than likely, they're going to put in the work to get freedom and healing, but the keyboard warriors are going to stay immature for a lifetime until they are forced to see their own hypocrisy and repent. They could stand to take Theodore Roosevelt's words to heart:

> It is not the critic who counts; not the man who points out how the strong man stumbles, or where the doer of deeds could have done them better. The credit belongs to the man who is actually in the arena, whose face is marred by dust and sweat and blood; who strives valiantly; who errs, who comes short again and again because there is no effort without error and shortcoming; but who does actually strive to do the deeds; who knows great enthusiasms, the great devotions; who spends himself in a worthy cause; who at the best knows in the end the triumph of high achievement, and who at the worst, if he fails, at least fails while daring greatly, so that his place shall never be with those cold and timid souls who neither know victory nor defeat.

If our response is anything other than prayer for our fallen brothers, sisters, fathers, and mothers, our hearts need to get right before the Lord. If we're shouting, "I SAW THAT COMING!" and we find our spirits tantalized to get sucked into scandal, I'd say that's a big red flag that something is not healthy in our souls. Discernment is a call to prayer. God showed you something because He trusted you to pray about it. If we'd rather feast on the shock of a fall than fall on our knees in intercession, we need to return to the cross.

When someone falls in the church, if we're not personally involved in their inner circle or process of restoration, prayer and checking up on our own garden are the only right responses. Anything beyond that is spiritualized gossip. Social media has somehow given us this wonky license to think we're entitled to an opinion about everything. I'm not sure we are. I'm not sure it's good for our souls to think we are.

"Dear brothers and sisters, if another believer is overcome by some sin, you who are godly should gently and humbly help that person back onto the right path. And be careful not to fall into the same temptation yourself."
—Galatians 6:1 (NLT)

"But I, the LORD, search all hearts and examine secret motives. I give all people their due rewards, according to what their actions deserve."
— Jeremiah 17:10 (NLT)

HOW TO RESPOND TO SCANDAL:
» Pray for those who are caught in sin, and be gentle.
» Check the health of your own heart.

- » Don't get sucked into detail mining and smear campaigns. We never know the full story.
- » Don't spiritualize slander and gossip. It still counts, even when it's used against the famous. If we're gossiping and not praying, we idolize scandals more than we care about the spiritual health of people.
- » Mind your business. We don't have to have the inside scoop or an opinion on everything. Two hundred years ago, we never would have known about most scandals if they weren't inside our close community. The World Wide Web is appropriately named. It connects us together, but too much connection can turn into a web, keeping us stuck in offense.

MINISTRY MOTIVES PERSONAL LITMUS TEST:
- » Would you still say yes to the call if it meant having a small influence but a large number of sons and daughters?
- » Do you turn down ministry opportunities without consulting the Lord because there's nothing in it for you?
- » Do you struggle to keep good works a secret?
- » Are there any areas you've stopped serving because it's felt beneath your title?
- » How do you feel when someone else gets credit for work you've done?
- » If nobody ever sees you do it, does it actually count?
- » Do you say yes to things without consulting the Lord because they have the potential to make you look good?

If we start measuring success by the size of our ministries or the length of our résumé, we're already in danger of not having a ministry to measure. Stop looking to the wrong altars. Stop begging God to do things in your life that are not resting on your life because you crave significance. Many times, our hearts ARE pure. We're excited and want people to celebrate Jesus with us. Valid. We want to spark faith, but when we let Jesus pierce our souls deeply with His loving gaze, it's *sometimes* because we secretly wanted to look significant.

JESUS ALONE SAVES SOULS. JESUS ALONE BUILDS HIS CHURCH.

If leading people to freedom or the masses to Jesus boosts your ego, you're working *for* love instead of *from* it—*for* identity instead of *from* it. Jesus alone saves souls. Jesus alone builds His church. I've learned to keep a knife on my flesh—ready to put Rhea to death anytime she starts to forfeit kingdom rewards on the altar of the praise of man.

It's hard because the mixture we've allowed into the church has normalized idolatry. If you feel the conviction of the Holy Spirit, here are a few practical shifts that could really help you walk out deliverance from professional Christianity and platform-building. As with all areas of our lives, nothing can be accomplished except through the blood of Jesus. We can make a formula out of just about anything, but the blood speaks a better word over all our striving.

7 TIPS TO PURIFY YOUR MOTIVES

1) Prep your heart more than your sermon.
2) Do secret works more than public ones.
3) Let other lips promote you instead of your own.
4) Go to the secret place after success.
5) Lean into God's feedback before you go to man.
6) Avoid the trap of comparison.
7) Keep five smooth stones of scripture in your sling to take out the giants of striving.

PIONEER PRAYER:

Jesus, wipe out even the fragrance of self-promotion hiding in my heart. Forgive me for the times I publicized the feet I washed and the chairs I sat in at the table. Forgive me for any way I've contributed to celebrity Christianity. I lay down the esteem of man and the idol I've made of influence. Help me not to cash in another reward on counterfeit significance. Let the "Well done" of heaven be enough to satisfy my soul. The only thing that matters on my résumé is that I belong to You. In Jesus's name. Amen.

Pioneer Prompt:

Get in a quiet place with the Lord, and tune out distractions. Think of Paul's résumé. It wasn't a list of achievements although He had plenty to brag about to the "super-apostles" he was conversing with. Instead, he preached his struggles, trials, and weaknesses. If you were to remove all the accomplishments attached to your name, what would be left on your résumé? Like Paul, preach your weaknesses. Use 2 Corinthians 11:22-30 as your template. Journal your response.

CHAPTER 5

The Woodchipper

I saw a video when I was scrolling through social media one day. An angry father tossed his son's video game console into a woodchipper, demanding his son work. The son refused. Without hesitation, pushing it down deeper into the woodchipper, the gift was chopped into bits. Then he grabbed another gaming console and asked the son again if he would work. Obviously, I don't know the context, but the son was basically manifesting idolatry and gaming addiction at this point and yelled something to the effect of: "Okay, I'll get a job!" It wasn't because he respected the father but because he didn't want to lose his gift.

ASSIGNMENTS CHANGE EVERY DAY, BUT THE GIFTS OF GOD RESTING ON YOUR LIFE ARE IRREVOCABLE.

Assignments change every day, but the gifts of God resting on your life are irrevocable. The moral of the story I shared is that God isn't tossing your gifts into the woodchipper when you don't exceed His expectations or even when you fail as a son. He's a *good* father. He's not in a hurry with your process. When we get sucked into striving and patterns of performance-based ministry, we stop working from love and start reaching for approval.

Romans 11:29 (ESV) says, "For the gifts and calling of God are irrevocable." The gifts of God are without repentance. That means that God will never regret giving them to you. He will never regret that He called you, and He will never take them back. Gifts can't be rescinded. If you've ever tried to return the wrong mail that went to your house, and it keeps showing up in your mailbox anyway, you know what I mean. The Greek word *charismata* means free, undeserved gifts. We can't lose what we didn't earn in the first place.

God won't take away gifts, but we *can* use them for the *wrong* kingdom. We see that with Judas. You can walk away from God, and you'll get to take your gift with you. Isn't that a heartbreaking and sobering thought? That we can build things without God and deny Him the very thing He wants most—*us?*

I remember seasons when God changed my assignment, and in my naivety, I thought that meant my calling was finished too. I didn't know there was a difference because I didn't understand Romans 11:29. Man can change your assignment, but nobody can change your calling. Our immaturity doesn't make God regret giving us gifts. He doesn't brood over our poor stewardship, although He will call us to give an account for it one day. Instead, He patiently trains us how to be *better* stewards.

This side of eternity, He gives as many second chances as we need. He doesn't flunk us. We just keep retaking the same test until we pass. And He always loves us. He couldn't stop loving you any more than He could separate from Himself. It's who He is. It's His nature to never stop loving you, but one day, we'll stand before Him, and it will be too late to repent. Taking advantage of grace is a risky game. It could mean the difference between heaven and hell—eternity with Him or forever separated from His presence. Choose *this* day. Not tomorrow. Not a better day when your life is cleaned up. *This one.* It's all we're promised. There is no condemnation in Christ. Only love.

God doesn't consult the accusers in your life to see if you're worthy of the gifts He's given you, any more than if Samuel had consulted Saul before anointing David or if God had consulted Herod to make sure it was a good time to send His Son. He isn't controlled or manipulated by man's offense, jealousy, or anger. There is so much safety to grow into full maturity under the covering of a kind and loving Father whose mercies are new every single day.

GOD WILL TEACH YOU HOW TO STEWARD WHAT YOU HAVE, BUT THIS REQUIRES US TO BE TEACHABLE.

No good father would give his toddler the car keys and say, "Go to town! See ya when you get back." Good fathers give the *right measure* of permission for the right season, and they stick with their children until they feel confident the gift will not hurt the child or others. He won't give you something that will destroy you without training you how to use it safely any more than we would hand our children a stick of dynamite and a match. God will teach you how to steward what you have, but this requires us to be teachable. He has to pressure-test our trustworthiness and character to see if we're ready, and then, He increases the anointing on it as we lean into the purifying fire of His love. Our daily choices determine if our gifts are oily or dry. He wants us dripping with the oil of His anointing.

No, my friend, God is not canceling your calling or throwing your gifts in the woodchipper because you blew it. Cancel culture is demonic. It's a preview of the separation of hell. It's a virus of slander spread by the prince of the air (Satan) through the airwaves (social media/chatter/gossip) to get us sucked into a swirl of second-heaven warfare. If you're wondering if it's seeped into the church, you bet it has! We haven't only tolerated it we've also *contributed* to it. We should have real concern for where things are headed. The enemy knows that if we can't love people we *do* see properly, we'll have a very hard time truly loving a God we can't see.

Those Jezebelic assignments won't be able to chase saints into isolation or stop the roar that's coming from the purified prophets. The sound will be a hammer blow to every old wineskin and clear the path for true reformation. You're going to rise above what tried to stomp you down. Let the roar of the Lion of the tribe of Judah be the loudest voice in your life. Cut the ties to every curse spoken over your destiny. Release the roar that's been manipulated and muzzled for far too long. The mantle is still there. It's up to you to pick it up and put it on.

Satan knows nothing of value can be accomplished in a house when the house is divided. He only has three goals: to steal, to kill, and to destroy. Therefore, if you find yourself thinking, *I wonder what Satan is doing today.* He is stealing, killing, and destroying—wherever there's an open door. He doesn't take vacations, and He doesn't retire, but he's clever enough to know never to sell it like that, or we would never receive it. So he packages it in more subtle things like spiritualized slander.

I was visiting the Museum of Science and Industry in Chicago the other day, and we were taking a tour of the actual captured German submarine U-505 from World War II. You could still smell the diesel fuel in the engine. (Strangely, it smells like crayons, if you were wondering.) As we were listening to the eerie sounds of the depth charge hitting the surface of the waves, we realized how far and fast and loud sound travels underwater. All anyone can do is hold their breath and wait for impact. As we squeezed in like sardines around the tight quarters, I learned a couple of things: First, people were a lot smaller in 1944. Second, the word subterfuge. I had never heard that word before. Subterfuge means to use deceit in order to achieve your goal. It comes from the Latin word *subterfugere* meaning "to escape secretly." I think this word perfectly describes how the accuser goes to war against the sons and daughters of God. Lots and lots of sabotage and trickery. Planting things in the dark, so they'll fall apart in the daylight. Moving around in the shadows, turning brother against brother, church against church.

It's interesting that Peter describes Satan as like a lion seeking someone to devour. Then Paul says in Galatians 5:15 (NLT), "But if you are always biting and devouring one another, watch out! Beware of destroying one another." I'd like to propose that, more often than not, the way Satan devours is through the tactic of subterfuge. We've gotten too comfortable fighting the wrong enemy while the real enemy continues to "escape secretly" back into the shadowy depths, laughing while we finish the job and devour each other.

WE'VE GOTTEN TOO COMFORTABLE FIGHTING THE WRONG ENEMY WHILE THE REAL ENEMY CONTINUES TO "ESCAPE SECRETLY" BACK INTO THE SHADOWY DEPTHS, LAUGHING WHILE WE FINISH THE JOB AND DEVOUR EACH OTHER.

I can attest to this tragedy from my own personal witness, but my biggest concern isn't being devoured, canceled, attacked, or rejected. *Jesus warned us that we would be.* (See John 15:18 for a reminder.) My biggest concern is the number of believers spiritualizing things that contradict Scripture. It's setting the stage for the antichrist. It's causing church splits and divisions. It's immature to throw people in the woodchipper and say it's from the Lord. It's deception, and it's time to grow up. Stop idolizing feelings and the flesh, and handle things biblically.

Cutting people we know out of our lives is super trendy on social media, but it's a VERY different gospel from the one Jesus preached. It's partnership with a spirit of rejection twisted and manipulated to look like a healthy, holy boundary. But healthy boundaries aren't spiritually abusive toward people. They don't isolate people from the body. They don't operate with a mob mentality. We cannot love people and devour them simultaneously and call it the kingdom.

There will never be a context from now until the end of time where the Bible doesn't apply to EVERY area of a believer's life. None of us have reached perfection, but this is a HUGE deception I see dividing people and houses of worship, friends, and families. If we do not address and remove this mixture of division and rejection in the church, many other sins, compromises, and messes will follow.

God entrusted us to be ministers of reconciliation, and He is going to hold us accountable to that one day and want a return on that investment, but all we're going to be able to hand Him is a pile of ashes from all the bridges we burned. How can we plead for people to reconcile with God when we can't even reconcile with each other? It grieves the Spirit to say we love God but hate our brother. It stops the flow of power. It opens the door to more demonic agendas when the enemy sees us not placing value in God's Word. I don't want to participate in Satan's subterfuge.

Not everyone is called to run with you forever. We have disagreements, diverging destinies, new seasons, and expiration dates on whom we link arms with, but none of that is reason to reject people. If you're in any level of relationship with people and you have offense, you are mandated by Scripture to go to that person privately and work it out biblically before you bring your offering to the Lord. God doesn't even want our worship until we clean up our messes with people!

HOW DID JESUS TREAT TAX COLLECTORS AND SINNERS? HE LEANED INTO RELATIONSHIP TO REDEEM THEM AND GIVE THEM NEW PURPOSE.

In Matthew 18, Jesus gives us a picture for dealing with sin in the church. Keep it private between the two of you. If the issue doesn't resolve that way, take witnesses. If the issue still doesn't get better, take it before the church. If they still don't listen, treat them like an unbeliever or tax collector.

Before we start thinking *that's* a loophole to cancel people, look at the interesting choice of words Jesus used. How did HE treat tax collectors and sinners? He leaned into relationship to redeem them and give them new purpose. It was always the religious Jesus was hardest on. When possible, we're called to live at peace with ALL people. One translation says to live as a friend to everybody. It's okay if you have to split ways, but do it hopefully and honorably, clearly communicating your boundary with people and leaving room for hope and reconciliation where possible.

Fear is a false protector. If I have to reject you to protect my heart, I have placed more faith in the enemy than God. Those walls you erect for your safety can easily become a prison if you don't add a bridge or a door. God can't honor dishonor in how we handle people, no matter how much the airwaves preach a different gospel. Healthy boundaries leave space for hope. Rejection leaves people hopeless, so what can we do?

> Do nothing from factional motives [through contentiousness, strife, selfishness, or for unworthy ends] or prompted by conceit and empty arrogance. Instead, in the true spirit of humility (lowliness of mind) let each regard the others as better than and superior to himself [thinking more highly of one another than you do of yourselves]. —Philippians 2:3 (AMPC)

Cancel culture has mixed into church culture. It's causing massive deception and so much division, destruction, pain, trauma, and confusion in the body. It's caused us to protect institutions instead of the people who are inside of them. Just about anywhere we look these days, you see a message that sounds spiritual but lacks a biblical foundation. It puffs us up with carnal thinking, but it leads to death. We have to fight for purity here. We cannot partner with hell and think we'll reap a harvest of kingdom fruit.

The world struggles to see Jesus if His bride is busy jealously devouring one another. Gossip will never pass for prayer in the courts of heaven. Jesus doesn't trust us with information on people if we're going to mishandle their hearts. He doesn't side with stone throwers, but He will regularly reveal our own junk if we humble ourselves enough to receive it.

Partnering with the accuser to assassinate churches or people based on feelings and not actual *fruit* is not prophetic or discerning; it's dangerously pharisaical. The language of hell is accusation. If you want to know what kingdom something is coming from, listen to the language. If I'm hearing everyone speak French, I can assume I'm in France. If I'm hearing everyone speak slander, I can assume it's coming from hell because heaven doesn't speak that language. The only thing we'll pioneer partnering with that language is new hellish ways to treat people.

Gossip can disguise itself as a lot of spiritual things: prayer, concern, discernment, etc. One thing it will never be is holy. God doesn't listen to accusation or bless it. His favor isn't on slander and subterfuge. Belittling someone else will never be your passport to promotion, and often, when we put our mouths on people with a hidden agenda to discredit them, God has a way of promoting *them* to humble *us*. We'll give an account to God one day for every single careless word we speak behind closed doors.

He will not honor a single moment of dishonor. This should evoke the fear of the Lord in how we conduct ourselves with other believers. I will never set out with a heart to reject people, but there are times we need to set a boundary.

SIGNS YOU NEED TO SET A BOUNDARY

» The fruit of someone's flesh is causing immense pain and harm to the church or to your family, and they are unwilling to repent or reconcile (or communicate about it biblically.)

» Their accusations are untrue to the fruit of our lives or the report of the Lord, but they refuse to believe truth and have already decided in their heart what they want

to believe and build a case out of their own delusions and deceptions.
» Their actions toward us have repeatedly been out of alignment with how Scripture teaches us to conduct ourselves in relationships. Instead, they spiritualize abuse, gossip, divisions, cruelty, backbiting, and slander, and make indirect assaults without coming to us personally.
» They don't want to be in an actual connected relationship with us but still follow along to plot against us, gossip, or lash out whenever they are triggered by an offense they came looking for.
» Anyone who says God told them anything that contradicts Scripture. God's voice does not contradict His Word. He's not going to show you all the dirt on someone else, but He'll regularly show you the plank in your own eye.

While we, on rare occasions, have had to block access, we never block love, forgiveness, honor, or a wholehearted desire to see others blessed—even those who wound and reject us. We don't speak curses heaven isn't speaking. We've simply chosen to focus on our own race and bless them as they focus on theirs. There was a time Paul and Barnabas had to go separate ways, but they didn't advance the kingdom of hell in how they did it.

Both were kingdom builders and apostolic encouragers. When Paul wanted to revisit all the cities from their first missionary journey to check on the health of the churches there, Barnabas (son of encouragement) loved the idea. Of course he did! But he wanted to take John Mark with them. Paul didn't want him to come since he had abandoned them in Perga.

Neither of them would change their opinion. It wasn't pride or arrogance. It was just different perspectives. Barnabas wanted to give it another shot. Paul didn't want to put him in the same situation again. So they agreed to disagree and instead of leaving the church, causing a church split with their division, stopping the work of the ministry from continuing, or pulling in people and making them pick sides instead of following Jesus—the kingdom of God multiplied in the middle of their division. They kept their issue personal. Barnabas and John Mark brought the gospel to Cyprus. Paul took Silas to Syria and Cilicia.

Here is my point: the kingdom of God can multiply *even* when we disagree. Don't allow a political spirit to harden your heart and cause your love to grow cold. Paul and Barnabas had different opinions. Both had sharp differing perspectives and disagreements. They took the gospel to different places and reached different people. Both kept their witness and honorably kept building His church.

DISAGREEMENT IS NOT THE GREATEST THREAT TO THE CHURCH. NOT KNOWING HOW TO DISAGREE HONORABLY IS.

Disagreement is not the greatest threat to the church. Not knowing how to disagree honorably is. *Unity* and *uniformity* are two very different concepts. One is kingdom, and the other is from hell. Our differences make us stronger. We confuse the enemy when we respond maturely in a climate of deception and divisiveness. Kingdoms are clashing; putting on the WHOLE Christ is our weapon. We can't keep fighting our battles like the world. We have to stay on the narrow road. Stop dieting on division. It's not free entertainment. An inability to kill our pride is more costly than we know. What you regularly feast on, you're giving access to be replicated in your own life.

Rejection is a revelation that you don't have God's perspective about a person or the maturity to kill your flesh. Far be it from us to say things about people heaven isn't saying. Create boundaries with the careful counsel of the Lord. If I ever do create a boundary with someone, I will likely attempt to work it out with them personally first or spend weeks or months even praying about it. It's never careless or emotionally charged. We need to follow Romans 12:18 (NIV): "As far as it depends on [us], live at peace with everyone." Reality is, though, that it doesn't always depend on us. If it depended on me, I wouldn't have any enemies. I hate conflict. But we are only responsible for the posture of our own hearts.

Many people need deliverance in our churches, and it should be our heart to help bring freedom to captives in the most loving way possible. We need to discern what's operating in an atmosphere, to evict that spirit, to rise above it, to establish and release the kingdom over that environment. We need to confront and correct in biblical, loving, safe, and God-honoring ways. First, God sent Elijah to prophesy the end of Jezebel. He then sent Jehu to finish the job. Sometimes, the battle coming against you isn't yours to end; it's just yours to start.

If you've experienced rejection or spiritual abuse, release it to Jesus. Cut those soul ties. Don't give the enemy one second of permission to hold you prisoner to the opinions of people who weren't in the room when He called you. Shake the dust of rejection off, and keep moving in the purposes of heaven. That's how you defeat Saul. You refuse to return the spears that were thrown to destroy you. That pit of rejection is likely the birthplace of your next promotion.

When people are wrestling with immaturity (like we all do at times) or even when they are under demonic influence, the only correct response is compassion, love, and prayer. Don't get sucked into second-heaven warfare by making battles about people or repaying evil with evil. Jesus is our best defense. Forgive. Forgive. FORGIVE. Seven times seventy times a day. A ridiculous amount of forgiveness to give away to match the ridiculous amount of forgiveness we've received. Forgiveness doesn't drag people through the mud. It doesn't punish, isolate, and reject. It doesn't blast offense to every listening ear. It doesn't get even. It keeps short records.

It covers. It protects. It gets over itself to celebrate what heaven sees in people. It collaborates in a beautiful agreement with heaven's heart. It ties the worst of what was done to the cross and hangs onto the best of who they are. That doesn't mean we'll sit at the same table this side of eternity, but it does mean we want you to feast on His goodness too. Renew your mind with the Word, worship, and the presence of God. This is protection from deception. It's hard to think thoughts heaven doesn't have when we have the mind of Christ about people.

And it starts by not throwing people in a woodchipper and not participating in subterfuge.

We dismantle the enemy when we handle ourselves biblically. We open ourselves to oppression when we don't. That means going to people privately when we've experienced a real offense. That means dying to our flesh every single day. You can cancel access without canceling love and honor for who people are in Christ and the value they add to the kingdom. Jesus could have canceled Judas, but instead, He washed his feet, broke bread with him, and kept His focus on the Father and the task assigned to Him.

JESUS COULD HAVE CANCELED JUDAS, BUT INSTEAD, HE WASHED HIS FEET, BROKE BREAD WITH HIM, AND KEPT HIS FOCUS ON THE FATHER AND THE TASK ASSIGNED TO HIM.

ROSE-COLORED HEART GLASSES

Rose-colored heart glasses. To see things like You do. I'm reminded when I wear them, I'm called to see people like You. Without love, we see things that are untrue. Take on someone else's offense. Misunderstand, slander, judge, abuse. Misrepresent Your heart and accuse. We only see and know in part. And when we start to think we know it all, we always miss Your heart. Whether our paths stay connected or purposefully apart. Love and honor are the kingdom way. Dishonor reveals the idols we've made. Of our own reputations. Our little kingdoms we defend. Forgetting we were supposed to be about His. These spectacles make a spectacle, Of the one who likes to accuse. Backbite, belittle, gossip, ghost, and wound. So he tried to swipe them off my face. And get me thinking on his level. But I have the mind of Christ, And I don't set a table for lying devils. My eyes are on Jesus. My focus is unhindered. Those arrows meant to take me out. Only made me more surrendered. I don't play games with pride. Or return the arrows meant to cut me alive. I don't see people after the flesh. I see them after the Spirit. And if Jesus isn't speaking death, I won't put my mouth against it. People can sound spiritual, And still think and act like hell. But the fruit of slander has a different smell. Like rotting relationships. Divided houses. Deceived hearts. Masquerading as discerning voices. We can think we're serving Jesus. But we switch kingdoms when we worship feelings. His voice never conflicts with His Word. If it does, go back and check what you heard. I don't receive labels that didn't come from Him. But I choose to speak blessings. And mean it with all I am. Offense is toxic and immature. I won't drink from poisoned waters. Or be led away from what's pure. There's no space held for unforgiveness. No time kept to resent. I will cheer you on from a distance. Even if you betray me up close with a kiss. When you learn to love your Judas, You finally start to look like Him. If you've been wounded, Jesus promised it would come. But when you respond like heaven. It makes the enemy run. Loving like Jesus doesn't mean I let you in. It's choosing to love you, release it, and forgive. —Rhea

I've noticed over the last few years, more than ever before, the accuser has been trying to build a team by sowing offense everywhere he can. It's concerning how many people he's drafting into his schemes. The moment we stop doing things God's way is the moment open season begins on the body of Christ. The war is getting too intense not to visit the threshing floor. The days Jesus warned us about are here. If we don't have love, we don't have anything. Remove love from the prophetic, love from the gifts, love from the ministry, and we're just a bunch of spiritualists with impressive gifts but no oil.

The enemy can't read our thoughts, but he can study our weaknesses. He keeps a file on our bloodline. Every time we walk in unrepentant sin, compromise, entertain gossip, carry offense and unforgiveness, and walk in hidden jealousy and pride, we teach him where our armor is weak. Don't live in fear, but also, let's not be ignorant.

When we stir up strife, judge and criticize, walk in hypocrisy, and believe the worst about people instead of the best, we have a very low value for what God values, and we're opening the door to the enemy. Leaders, you can't ignore these attitudes in your churches. They aren't innocent. Deal with them biblically, or they won't stop until they take your whole house down.

Avoiding biblical confrontation never produces holy fruit. If we have a problem with someone, we need to tell them privately like the Bible says. But before we do that we need to filter our offense through the Holy Spirit. Our feelings are our own to own. We are not called to walk around feeling victimized by everything people do that hurts our feelings. That's an exhausting way to live. For you and for others. We need to place high value on that which heaven values. It's spiritually abusive to hurt people and call it love. Heaven values honor and love—honor for the least, honor for the leader, and honor for every person in between.

HEAVEN VALUES HONOR AND LOVE—HONOR FOR THE LEAST, HONOR FOR THE LEADER, AND HONOR FOR EVERY PERSON IN BETWEEN.

If we're using our gifts as a weapon to manipulate, brainwash, intimidate, sow fear, flatter, or control people, we've crossed over kingdom lines, and we need to repent, get clean, and come home. There are times people preach, and it steps on my toes, but it's biblical, so I know it's not them attacking me. It's the Holy Spirit *convicting* me, and it's a gift to make me more like Christ.

Let's stop throwing people in the woodchipper, and focus on the real enemy. We need to mature in our discernment if we think people are the problem. There is a spiritual battle all around us. Let's not build cases in our hearts against people or adopt other people's offense as our own. Let's love people deeper than that. Let's fight harder to cover offense. There is a way that *seems* right and a way that *is* right. The Lord knows the difference. Jesus warned us of all the darkness we'd face in these days, but His biggest concern was that we'd lose our love—our love for Him and our love for one another. Sometimes, we get more zealous about removing demons than we do about protecting what really is most precious to Him. Love.

We need to stop being a "safe place" for people to bring gossip and slander. It's one of the biggest deceptions the enemy tries to get us to take lightly. We have a mandate from heaven to be like Jesus and to see people as heaven sees them. This is one of many reasons consumerism in the church is contributing to so much pain and destruction and causing people to deconstruct their faith with no intent of ever reconstructing it. I don't desire at all to sound harsh or condemning because many churches that fly the banner of family operate with the heart of the Father. I don't want to discredit those houses at all or the fruit of their intentionality. However, in many other instances, churches market themselves to be "family" because it attracts consumers, and too often, what people really get is control and manipulation. We overpromise and underdeliver. At best, they get a very toxic dysfunctional family and years of therapy to try and untangle the web of confusion. Sauls create orphans. Fathers create sons.

If the fruit of our lives is death and division, it didn't come from Jesus. It's a manifestation of our immaturity and an orphan spirit operating in our ministries. It's a billboard for how well we listen to the devil and how little we understand sonship. Too many churches have son language and orphan hearts. Sauls operating in an orphan spirit attract a whirlwind of warfare. They suck you in with their vision and charisma and then leave a trail of destruction in the aftermath because orphans only truly care about one thing *promoting themselves at the expense of everything that they see as a threat to their end goal.* Orphans are always thinking of numero uno and it's the undercurrent of everything they produce for the kingdom. But the good news is we don't have to stay immature. There is always room to repent, grow, and go the Jesus way. If you've been a Saul or have been hurt by one—forgive, bless, and release the offense. When we fight our own battles, we forfeit our right to heaven's protection.

As I've mentioned, some people show up in your life already fully committed to believing the worst—not because you did anything wrong but because they see the anointing resting on your life as a threat to the throne they sit on. The jealousy and hidden agendas hiding in their hearts will cause them to use slander to keep others from connecting with your ministry. It will force them to always try to one-up everything you do. You pray. They pray louder. Sons operate in simplicity because they recognize the Source. Think Elijah. Orphans operate through striving. Think prophets of Baal.

Someone with an orphan spirit does not sit well under anyone else's leadership. They are ready to reject others before they themselves are rejected. They need constant validation. They are squirmy if they're not the most important person in the room. They will even claim gifts that they do not operate in just because they want what you have instead of being content with what they have. They will take credit for fields you plowed while your hands are blistered and theirs are as smooth as a baby. You can discern this because the fruit will be bad. Before we get judgmental of those under the influence of an orphan spirit, it's important to remember that the older brother in the prodigal son story behaved like an orphan too. He was unnecessarily working as a slave for love. *"All these years I slaved for you. I did everything right. You never gave me a young goat to feast with my friends."* Jesus carried the weight of our orphanhood on the cross so that we could forever identify as fully accepted sons and daughters.

PEOPLE OPERATING FROM SONSHIP ARE UNFAZED BY ALL OF THE SUBTERFUGE BECAUSE THEIR IDENTITY IS SO ROOTED IN THE LOVE OF THE FATHER THAT THERE IS ABSOLUTELY NOTHING AN ORPHAN CAN DO TO STOP THEM FROM BEING A SON.

There's a tangible difference between the language and ministry of sons and orphans, but if you don't know how to distinguish the difference, you might just be left with a conflicted feeling around that person and not even know why it's there. After all, an orphan spirit operating in a church looks spiritual and sounds spiritual, but it always leans toward subtle attempts at self-promotion. And truthfully, people operating from sonship are unfazed by all of the subterfuge because their identity is so rooted in the love of the Father that there is absolutely nothing an orphan can do to stop them from being a son. You can even take away their assignment, and they shake the dust off and keep moving forward. You can try and sabotage their oil or taint it with offense, but it stays pure because sons give orphans NO access.

A leader operating with an orphan spirit will partner with the accuser to try and put a lid over your calling, lock you out of rooms you've been called to, dig up dirt to disqualify your voice, and take credit for things you built because they view sons as a threat to their portion. They will seek to supplant and usurp you and often can cause a lot of death, division, and damage in the church before they get exposed and move on to the next unknowing house or team. When you don't deal with an orphan spirit operating in your church biblically, they can infect the sheep who are too new or naive to know any better. What's most alarming is that every bit of the destruction is done under the guise of love, care, concern, and spirituality. It's toxic. It's dangerous. Run, do not walk, from leaders who make excuses for these behaviors because, somehow, they are benefiting from them, often at *your* expense.

I had a dream a few years ago that I was walking over a hill to get a drink from a river. Along the shores of the river were dead bodies and animals scattered everywhere. The water looked beautiful and inviting. Clean. Cool. Clear. Refreshing even. But I knew not to drink the water because it had been poisoned with offense. If I had just focused on the water and ignored the wreckage, I would have been another dead body.

My dream was a warning to the church: be careful what stream you're drinking from. We need discernment. Not everything is as it seems. Look around, and judge the fruit. Be careful not to just see what you want to see and miss the protection of God. If the fruit is death, God is not the source. If the behavior is not Christ-like, God is not the source. Looking back, there are several moments when the fruit was obvious, but I saw what I wanted to see. Had I leaned into that discernment, it would have saved me a lot of trauma from people who claimed to be from the Spirit but actually were producing fruit in keeping with the opposite kingdom. When consumerism is elevated above Christlikeness, hellish fruit will always be the outcome. They attract the warfare swirling around them by the doors they open and the kingdom they partner with—and it's not always intentional. Anytime we move outside of Scripture, we are wide open to deception.

I have seen the orphan spirit poison the river, split the most honoring of houses, and turn even the closest of friends into overnight enemies. Matthew 18:7 (author paraphrase) has something to say about that, though: "But woe to the man by whom the offense comes." Don't drink the water the accuser is serving, no matter how pure it looks. It will destroy the purity of your love for people. It will fog the lens of how you see them. You cannot find kingdom things outside of kingdom principles. There's only one group that belongs in the woodchipper, and that's Satan and his demons.

THERE'S ONLY ONE GROUP THAT BELONGS IN THE WOODCHIPPER, AND THAT'S SATAN AND HIS DEMONS.

I walked through a season of the most hellish warfare I've ever witnessed in my life as this spirit operated in the lives of believers. I overcame by the mercy of God (and a lot of healing and counseling) with my love and purity intact. We gain authority over the battles we win. I've been tossed in the woodchipper dozens and dozens of times. They say most people lose up to seven close relationships in their lifetime. For pastors, it's something like seven a year. I walked through a three-year period when I had to stop tracking how many people walked away due to a spirit of accusation. I'm a pretty honest judge of my own fruit and character and repent quickly when I contribute to offense. But guys, when I tell you this was like the most bizarre warfare I've ever experienced, I'm not lying. None of it was handled biblically or based on fruit I could fix. The enemy was assaulting our character by giving people we loved demonic dreams and visions, telling them lies to sow fear and break connection.

Trusted voices in our life, who were trying to shut down the insanity of that season, let us know that people were gossiping and accusing me of being a Jezebel, being a witch, being the opposite of everything true to the fruit of my life. If I would even open my mouth and speak against this spirit, they would double down on their resolve to assault my character. Key players were instigating what I refer to now as the Great Exodus. We can't control what comes against us but refusing to heal because of it, is unacceptable. You are worth healing.

Looking back now, I realize nobody actually has the power to assault my character because I died to my reputation long before they had an opinion about it. I picked up my cross and put down my right to carry offense. We can't carry both. But this wasn't our enemies attacking us. That could be expected. It was the people we invested our whole lives into serving and caring for. People we lost sleep over. People we fasted with. People we saw miracles with. People we broke bread with around our table. People we loved were just ghosts we used to know. It was like there was no time to even come up for oxygen. I'd finally process one grief, and then another would come. And another. And another. Isn't that worth holding onto offense? *No. Never.*

You never expect the people in your own foxhole to turn their guns on you. You begin to wonder if the love and camaraderie were ever even real. But we leave those unanswerable questions at the cross. It was too much to keep up with and not a burden we were called to bear. It got to the point that if someone we loved suddenly disappeared, and we couldn't reflect upon anything we may have done to cause it, we could just assume the gossip and accusation had poisoned their river. This time, I had the boundaries and mindsets in place to not let it immobilize me.

If you trace the fruit to the root, you will find the accuser behind *every* accusation and his messengers are often offended believers. God doesn't speak a language of condemnation and division. Only the devil does that. But if we steward our pain well, that place of attack can become the birthplace of purpose. My heart in sharing is not to contribute to any dishonor in the retelling of my experience but to bring freedom to others walking through a similar situation. I know that I am not unique to this type of warfare. What I am sharing won't change or prevent what's coming against you, but hopefully, it will give you tools to not be crushed under the weight of it and to actually gain new levels of freedom *because* of it.

IF YOU TRACE THE FRUIT TO THE ROOT, YOU WILL FIND THE ACCUSER BEHIND EVERY ACCUSATION.

God promises in His Word that the comfort we receive from Him will be the same comfort we're able to carry to others. That's the power of your story. It can pull people out of a pit. He writes redemption into every line for that *very* purpose. Your healing is in motion and even in the process; your story is already helping others get freedom. Trauma isn't getting the spotlight. Jesus is. In the hands of Jesus, your trauma becomes a testimony to HIS glory that strengthens others in their time of testing.

Your testimony is a hammer in the hands of a holy God. It's dripping with the oil of breakthrough for someone about to *break* through. You may be reading this, and you just feel like you're breaking apart. Your family is breaking apart. Your friendships and purpose are breaking apart. No—you're breaking *through*. There is a difference. But you won't fully believe me until you get to the other side and see for yourself. If I'm speaking to anyone, hold on. You're almost through it, and I promise if you keep your heart postured in forgiveness and humility, you'll even grow because of what tried to take you out!

You've probably heard the phrase, "The enemy doesn't rob empty houses." It is true. He knows where the oil is, and he goes after things that carry value. But He also loves to come set up shop in empty houses, so it's important to stay full of the Spirit. I know it sounds like fluff to make you feel good, but the reality is that if you're pursuing the things of God, the opposition coming against you is less about you and more about what's in your house.

Jezebelic witchcraft slander assigned to take you out can cause irrational fear and is keen on character assassination. It makes you want to give up your calling and seeks to muzzle your voice. It causes isolation, discouragement, depression, confusion, and fatigue. It makes you feel alone, even though you're not alone. It causes you to operate in the fear of man and be hypervigilant not to say or do anything that might ruffle feathers. You have full permission and access through Christ to rebel against these demonic assignments trying to oppress you. The fear of the Lord protects you from the fear of man.

You're coming out of the wilderness holy, prepared, and filled with the fuel of personal revival. God is releasing justice over the havoc and anguish the enemy has launched against you in the last season. He is redeeming lost time and giving you the mind of Christ where there has been wave after wave of mental torment. This demonic agenda will have no more access to your destiny. We command it to go in Jesus's name. What you carry isn't just a move—it's an expression of the heart of the Father on the earth. The massive retaliation and war against your voice is because you're closer now than you've ever been to walking through a door of destiny. So take heart from Proverbs 28:1 (NLT): "The wicked run away when no one is chasing them, but the godly are as bold as lions."

The enemy is behind every attack, but he will often use people to carry it out—even people we love and do life with whose eyes have been blinded and consciences seared. People we shared meals with around our table but have rejected truth. The enemy wouldn't waste his time if these were superficial, shallow relationships. But take heart because not one single fiery arrow of jealousy, gossip, or slander will hit the mark. You are positioned under an open heaven. You will occupy the land. You will see the promise come to pass.

Your circle may get small, but the people who are called to be there will stay. Jesus had three. Sometimes, God gets things really small for a season because He's about to increase *you* and everyone around you. He may not rebuild that relationship, but He will always rebuild *you*. The rejection you're struggling to overcome very likely could have been the protection of the Lord. Sometimes, He has to unyoke you from people with agendas you can't see. Let Him.

The accuser can divide a house. He can sow complete delusion as though it's reality overnight. But his ability to destroy will never overpower God's ability to restore. I never understood how Elijah could be so irrationally afraid of Jezebel after so much victory until I faced the same spirit and realized its influence in the life of believers. I get it now. Running for his life through the wilderness into caves of isolation . . . not so far-fetched. Angels have to come minister because you don't even have the strength to eat. I get it.

We've experienced a lot of warfare against our calling as a family. If you're pioneering anything pure for Jesus, you probably have some battle scars too. It's the anointing that breaks yokes. It's the anointing on your life he wants to shut down. When yokes need to be broken, you better believe he's not firing his arrows at the ones with empty lamps. He's coming for those on the battlefield who are carrying oil. The weapon will forge, but it will not prosper.

I DO NOT THINK GOD INTENDED US TO DEPEND MORE ON DELIVERANCE THAN ON THE DELIVERER.

You can expect intense warfare when you are a prophetic voice that discerns red flags and releases God's heart into atmospheres that need reformation. But there is a type of hyperfocus on demonic activity that has gotten dangerous and a little wonky in the church. I do not think God intended us to depend more on deliverance than on the Deliverer. Remember what I said earlier? What has our focus has our worship.

We've been focused a lot on warfare in this chapter, and it's really important to pause and clarify that the activity of devils will never be more impressive than Jesus. Please do not make demonic activity the main conversation. I'm not promoting ignorance to spiritual battles, but memorizing every name of every demon isn't going to lead anyone closer to Jesus. I've encountered people who can't even carry on a normal conversation with the hurting and broken without pointing out every spirit operating behind this, that, or the other. Sometimes, we just need to sit in silence with people and love them like Jesus.

If you begin to discern and try to shepherd people through areas of false teaching and error and immaturity, don't be surprised if you're met with some surprising and intense resistance. Not just from the people you're trying to help but from the covert spirit operating behind those deceptions. Anytime you see error causing damage and division in the church there needs to be gentle, loving, biblically based correction, whether it comes from a pastor or another father or mother in the house. Not properly shepherding these gifts operating in a church can cause a lot of damage.

When healthy, deliverance ministry has the ability to lead people into encounters with the Father's love and freedom. If you don't believe in deliverance, you don't believe in the gospel. If you're not familiar with the Bible, deliverance is mentioned A LOT. Deliverance is a biblical mandate for ALL believers, according to Matthew 10:8 (NIV): "Heal the sick, raise the dead, cure those with leprosy, and cast out demons."

God has regularly killed my flesh, disciplined my immaturity, and delivered me from bondage. But I've also experienced shocking attacks and retaliation from the enemy for discerning and exposing places of error he wanted to stay hidden. Sometimes, demons that have been hiding for a long time in an institution or region retaliate when you find their hiding hole. They masquerade as angels of light with small additions of or subtractions from truth. There's just enough contradiction that you have to really know the Word of God to even notice them.

Things get weird when we try to cast out the flesh, counsel demons, or deliver people from immaturity. Knowing what battle you're fighting is like step one of fighting a battle. A lot of things are demonic and need dealing with as such. Jesus gave us authority for that. We need to discern the spirit operating behind things. But if you think *everything* is a demon, that's going to cause some damage—especially if you're operating in the pride and error of thinking you're the answer to every person's spiritual problems and that your discernment is infallible. Nothing causes people to bring out the woodchipper like exposing an area of pride in their ministries or the problem with the sacred cows they've made of them.

Anytime we become more infatuated with what the devil is doing than what heaven is doing, we've started switching kingdoms. Clearly, demons are real and should be dealt with, and we have authority through the blood to cast them out. But demons will never be a better topic than Jesus. People who like to talk about demons more than Jesus probably have them. Hanging out with people who are infatuated by demon activity is not a good plan. Things get weird fast when people build theology around demons instead of Jesus. We need better discernment than that.

The enemy loves attention, and he wants to be the center of it. That's why he was cast out of heaven. So if the bulk of what people are focused on is demonic activity, isn't that giving him exactly what he wanted from the start? Our eyes? Focused on him? I'd be concerned if we *weren't* casting demons out of our churches, but I'd be equally concerned if all we were ever doing was casting demons out of our churches. Why is your church so demonized is a better question. Why are so many demons feeling comfortable in your gatherings?

LITMUS TEST FOR HEALTHY DELIVERANCE MINISTRY:
- » Am I actually dealing with a demon or immaturity?
- » Does this person need to be discipled or delivered?
- » Is this a flesh issue or a demon issue?
- » How can I equip this person to stay free?
- » Does this person need professional counseling?
- » Am I partnering with Satan and missing Jesus?
- » Does this lead people to Jesus or to my ministry?

I want to be empathetic and gentle in what I'm about to say. If a person is stepping into deliverance rooms on a weekly basis over an extended period of time, I think there may be a lack of teaching on how much permission, access, and authority the enemy actually has in the life of a believer. Jesus discipled disciples and delivered demons.

We need truth AND love to accurately represent the Father while seeing error removed. If you've hit a nerve and stepped into a woodchipper of warfare, have a game plan for the retaliation you're likely to experience as a result of it. You can't control what other people do or say, but blocking access to the voice of the accuser could mean the difference between life and death.

HOW TO DISMANTLE SMEAR CAMPAIGNS LAUNCHED AGAINST YOU:
- » Pull a safe pastor or mentor into the situation.
- » Avoid peer-to-peer gossip.
- » Keep the damage zone minimal. Don't empower the smear campaign by spreading your offense to others.

- » Do not retaliate or try to clear your name.
- » Let the truth and the fruit defend your reputation.
- » Rebuke the assignment and renounce the lie.
- » Nourish your body and soul. Eat and rest well.
- » Bless those who persecute you. Forgive them.
- » Worship. Stay in the Word. Stay in family. And do NOT shut down your voice and calling for anyone.
- » Prepare to advance because you postured yourself for promotion by responding properly.

I've experienced the woodchipper from people who were operating in accusation and bore fruit in keeping with it. As simple as these strategies from the Lord are not only were they boundaries protecting my heart from emotionally charged reactions, but also, they were passports to my promotion. (I get Joseph; not everyone is as excited to hear our dreams as we are to tell them.)

I've experienced people scrutinizing every move I made, word I spoke, or dream I shared, and either putting their stamp of approval or disapproval on it in an attempt to control the flow of my oil. *As if their approval even matters.* People that I don't even do life with would pick up secondhand offense through gossip and block me, comment nasty things on my posts, or slide into my DMs and tell me off for using my platform to encourage and edify the church. Everything I did was being viewed through a filter of accusation. Things are always watered down as information travels through the gossip wireless. Each retelling of the story is more polluted than the last.

Back to the submarine story I mentioned earlier in this chapter. As we were in a tight, confined passageway, the tour guide couldn't point out everything to everybody at the same time. So she said, "Let's play the telephone game. Whatever I say, tell the person behind you." I was second in line, so I clearly communicated what the tour guide said to the person behind me because I heard it firsthand, but the message fell apart the farther down the line it went. By the time the information got to the very last person, it was completely distorted. This is how accusation travels through gossip.

I could regale you with story after story of the spears I've survived in that season and throughout my lifetime. The details would make your stomach turn, but that's not going to be happening because that's not the goal of this book. I'm not contributing to any more division or any narrative or internal dialogue where the enemy gets me thinking and behaving like a victim or an orphan. It's just super essential that we remember the Word is a sword. Dividing soul and spirit. Bone and marrow. Thoughts and motives. We aren't the sword, and if we try to be, people get hurt. If it does cut, you're not the cause. It's the nature of a sword.

Someone bringing gentle and loving correction to error through all the correct biblical channels is not an attack on your ministry. Humility and teachability are markers of maturity. Sometimes, the warfare that's trying to kill you, God will actually use to form you if you let Him. The enemy will try to hijack your wilderness and transform it into an excuse to quit. You have the authority to reject any wilderness the enemy has counterfeited to make you feel abandoned by God in order to derail your destiny. The wilderness is God's design. Satan can't have it! The torment ends now. God was not the author of that season of confusion.

THE WILDERNESS IS GOD'S DESIGN. SATAN CAN'T HAVE IT! THE TORMENT ENDS NOW. GOD WAS NOT THE AUTHOR OF THAT SEASON OF CONFUSION.

In the middle of reformation, the real battle isn't between people but between the old wineskin and the new. Not everyone will be able to hold onto the wave. But we don't make kingdom shifts with the goal of pleasing people. We're called to obedience to our assignment. Many who start with you won't be called to finish with you, and that's when we bless and release them. If you did it for Jesus, none of it was wasted. Maybe the battle you're experiencing is less about a person and more a war over where God wants to take you *next* and the ones coming up after you:

> "And who pours new wine into an old wineskin? If someone did, the old wineskin would burst and the new wine would be lost. New wine must always be poured into new wineskins. Yet you say, 'The old ways are better,' and you refuse to even taste the new wine that I bring." —Luke 5:37-39 (TPT)

And how did Jesus respond to the Pharisees:

> But when the Pharisees heard about the miracle, they said, "No wonder he can cast out demons. He gets his power from Satan, the prince of demons." Jesus knew their thoughts and replied, "Any kingdom divided by civil war is doomed. A town or family splintered by feuding will fall apart. And if Satan is casting out Satan, he is divided and fighting against himself. His own kingdom will not survive. And if I am empowered by Satan, what about your own exorcists? They cast out demons, too, so they will condemn you for what you have said. But if I am casting out demons by the Spirit of God, then the kingdom of God has arrived among you. —Matthew 12:24-28 (NLT)

When the Pharisees tried to demonize Jesus, He didn't run. He publicly rejected labels that didn't come from His Father, kept His eyes on the task at hand, and gives us permission to do the same. If you've ever experienced that kind of hellish rejection, I'm so sorry. Whatever the rejection or accusation, stay anchored in the truth that none of that love was wasted, and none of those years were lost if it was done for Jesus. The fruit of your obedience still counts in heaven, even if people toss it away. I'm a fiercely loyal friend, but I've had to learn that some people are only meant to stay in our lives for a season.

Clinging to those relationships would actually hold you back and take up space when God is wanting to make room for the *new thing* He is bringing into your life. It still hurts, though, and we need to properly grieve those lost friendships. Nobody gets that suffering like Jesus. He washed the feet that would walk away from Him too because:

> "A tree is identified by its fruit. If a tree is good, its fruit will be good. If a tree is bad, its fruit will be bad. You brood of snakes! How could evil men like you speak what is good and right? For whatever is in your heart determines what you say. A good person produces good things from the treasury of a good heart, and an evil person produces evil things from the treasury of an evil heart. And I tell you this, you must give an account on judgment day for every idle word you speak. The words you say will either acquit you or condemn you." —Matthew 12:33-37 (NLT)

HOW TO PROCESS PROPHETIC WORDS:
- » Test them against Scripture. (Galatians 1:8)
- » They need to bear witness to the receiver. (Proverbs 2:2)
- » They should reflect the fruit of your life. (Matthew 12:33)
- » They should align with the insight of mothers and fathers who know you. (Hebrews 13:17)
- » They should accurately represent God's heart for you. (John 3:17)
- » They shouldn't cause divisions. (Jude 1:19)
- » They should be interpreted through the Holy Spirit, not fallible human filters. (2 Peter 1:20-21)
- » They should comfort, edify, and exhort. (1 Corinthians 14:3)

If the word doesn't measure up, then you may be dealing with an accusation ministry instead of a discernment ministry, and you have the biblical obligation to lovingly take that word and flush it down the toilet as fast as possible. When people say their discernment isn't wrong, you have a responsibility to mark that word because infallibility is not scriptural. (See 1 Corinthians 13:9.) In the new covenant, we mark words, not people. (See 1 Corinthians 14:29.)

We love people. We LOVE people. We. Love. People. We don't reject them, but we can reject a word. And we should when it's not flowing from the throne of God. We value words and the people who deliver them to us, but we also have the ability and spiritual responsibility to hear God's voice for ourselves and test *all* things to Scripture.

WE VALUE WORDS AND THE PEOPLE WHO DELIVER THEM TO US, BUT WE ALSO HAVE THE ABILITY AND SPIRITUAL RESPONSIBILITY TO HEAR GOD'S VOICE FOR OURSELVES AND TEST ALL THINGS TO SCRIPTURE.

You can't partner with the accuser *and* see people like Jesus. They are contradicting news reports. You will believe one and despise the other. You will get more of what you focus on, and what you don't focus on will get lost. When offense and accusation are not dealt with biblically, you better believe the courtroom will be filled with people poisoned against you until Defender Jesus walks in and says, "Case closed." The only truth is heaven's perspective. Don't believe slander staged to discredit other believers. Judge fruit for yourself, keep short accounts, and conduct yourselves biblically. Gossip should die when it knocks on our door. If it lives, it's because the enemy brought it to a house he knew he could depend on.

If that's you, listen to James:

> Confess and acknowledge how you have offended one another and then pray for one another to be instantly healed, for tremendous power is released through the passionate, heartfelt prayer of a godly believer! —James 5:16 (TPT)

I have nothing but love, honor, and compassion for every person who knowingly or unknowingly partnered with the accuser to cause me and my family harm throughout our decades in ministry. I fear the Lord too much to hold onto offense. I pray nothing but blessings and favor over them and their ministries. I pray they mature and increase in every way. I pray the Lord shines His face upon them, their families, and their future. I pray they experience the fullest measure of the goodness of God. I will not spend a second of my life yoked to bitterness, offense, or malice.

Sometimes, people are still growing in their gifts, and if you write someone off based on where they start, you're going to miss the beautiful fruit of how they mature and finish. I've made some ugly messes as I was learning to use my gifts too. Never judge someone's future based on their history. Wait and see how the Lord turns it around for good. Not one arrow will prosper. Not one accusation will stick. You will flourish in the house of the Lord. So will they. You will increase in every way. So will they. But it starts with forgiveness:

> Jesus said, "Pay attention to yourselves! If your brother sins, rebuke him, and if he repents, forgive him, and if he sins against you seven times in the day, and turns to you seven times, saying, 'I repent,' you must forgive him." —Luke 17:3-4 (ESV)

Jesus loves our enemies as much as He loves us. Not everything gets reconciled this side of heaven, and there are some people who, if you didn't set a boundary, could cause real damage to your life. But we can certainly thank Jesus for the value every single person has added to our lives, even if they were only there for a season. The people who caused me the most pain accelerated my maturity and deepened my roots. They actually served God's plan to help me level up.

Even if the only thing of value someone added to your life was a boundary that had been missing, it's never *ALL* bad, friends. Make sure you remember that in the retelling of history. Cherish the beauty. Don't ever reduce a person down to your discernment of them or their past failures. Partnering with the accuser is switching kingdoms.

YOU CAN LIVE IN REACTION TO THE GOODNESS OF GOD OR IN REACTION TO THE ACTIVITY OF THE DEVIL, BUT THE TWO WILL ALWAYS BE IN CONFLICT.

You can live in reaction to the goodness of God or in reaction to the activity of the devil, but the two will always be in conflict. We give the enemy too much influence and credit. Jesus was continually around demonic activity. He dealt with it. He taught us how to deal with it. But His focus was always on the Father. We can't bring kingdom solutions to first-heaven issues when we're caught up in second-heaven warfare. Going toe to toe with demons and man is not a battle we were called to fight. We war from the high place—that third-heaven place seated with Christ in heavenly places where Jesus already won every battle.

People may partner with the enemy, but the real enemy of your soul is always Satan. The season of warfare you're walking through may feel like it's never going to stop, but it will. Choosing to die on mountains you weren't called to will take you out fast. That's a place where wisdom goes to die. That's where the flesh gets so loud we can't hear the gentle whisper of the Holy Spirit inviting us to let it go and trust Him to fight the battle. God sees, and God fights for those who give up the right to fight for themselves.

When you fight spiritual battles with human weapons, people get hurt. Someone might be one more arrow away from never returning to hope. Don't treat people like garbage. Don't be that person that hides behind a mask of spirituality but wounds people by not keeping your ego in check or living it out in the fruit of your actions. I've been that person. You've probably been that person.

Suspicion isn't prophesy. It's glorified fear. Orphans operate from fear. Prophetic gifts should seek God's heart through

Scripture and a lens of love and redemption for ALL people. It produces good fruit, while accusation has really dangerous fruit that puts people against each other and causes a lot of division and pain. Whatever we do for the Lord, we have to also be willing to receive His correction and repent when we misuse it. I don't know the source of the quote, but it makes me laugh because it's so true: "Nobody cares if you speak in tongues if you're mean in English."

Let's stop magnifying the speck in other people's eyes and missing the giant plank in our own. Our petty drama and hypocrisy make the lost want nothing to do with Jesus. Whatever you magnify, you're going to get more of. Ever notice how offended people find each other in a group? That's not an accident. The enemy is an expert at turning a tiny offense not handled biblically into a giant echo chamber of division.

There's been so much spiritual abuse, slander, and gossip launched like arrows at MANY in the body of Christ as attempts to assault His image-bearers and to shut down through confusion and distraction the birthing of what God has been dreaming to release on the earth through our laid down lives. To add clarity, correction from the Lord is not an arrow, and it's not an attack on your ministry. There is a difference. Not everything that hurts your feelings is from hell. Orphans view correction as punishment. Sons embrace it as love.

NOT EVERYTHING THAT HURTS YOUR FEELINGS IS FROM HELL. ORPHANS VIEW CORRECTION AS PUNISHMENT. SONS EMBRACE IT AS LOVE.

I was watching *The Hobbit*[6] one day. It was the scene where Bilbo and the dwarves got lost in Mirkwood Forest on their way to the lonely mountain. They were no longer able to think clearly. The atmosphere was thick with confusion and heavy, HEAVY oppression. It was causing them to turn against each other, fall asleep in poisoned waters, and go in circles never making progress. They should really have called that forest "Jezebel Forest" because that's exactly what it's like dealing with that spirit. So, Bilbo began to climb higher. He made it above the oppression and breathed the clean air of freedom while butterflies symbolically fluttered around him. And he could see where they had to go from here. I find it very appropriate that butterflies are waiting at the top. Nobody understands the pain of metamorphosis like a butterfly. They literally turn themselves into goop in the safety of their chrysalis before they emerge solid and ready to sore. Your pain is a good qualifier to walk the broken into a new day.

It's time to breathe the fresh air again. The sword of His Word, the oil of His presence, living inside of your purpose, and having the right people around you can protect you from fighting a lot of battles you're not called to fight. All that slander straight from the pit is BREAKING OFF of your mind.

As I was watching this scene it was such a prophetic picture of what I have personally experienced and witnessed. As you get freedom here, I believe that you're even going to see some of the unexplained physical symptoms begin to lift off of you. Some of you are going to feel like you're breathing for the first time. Your energy will come back. The fog and confusion will

---
6 *The Hobbit*, directed by Peter Jackson (2012; New York, NY: New Line Cinemas).

lift from around your mind. The tightness in your shoulders and chest will release. Body aches, high blood pressure, and digestive issues will be healed. The breakthrough you've been contending for is here.

It's time to step out of that very oppressive spiderweb forest where it's been easy to get entangled in the affairs of demons and men and hard to get a solid footing. But it's like every time you've tried to climb higher, you've slipped and stayed stuck in the slime of slander. Stuck where the air has been thick with deception, confusion, and fatigue. Where you're getting caught in webs of sticky sabotage. It's time to climb up above the trees and breathe again. He is making you sure-footed for the climb. It's time to climb higher, beloved.

It's time to remember who you *really* are again before the enemy used people to confuse you about your true identity. The Father has always known the real you. He was never confused. It's time to see all the butterflies of transformation and meet YOU 2.0. You're an oil carrier. You're a curse breaker. You're a purified prophetic voice. You're a pioneer priest. You're a loved son or daughter.

The only right way to rediscover YOU is to look at HIM. The world looks inward; the church is called to look UPWARD. It's time to see from the high place seated with Christ in heavenly places where every battle is under His feet. It's time to rescue those seduced by doctrines of demons, weary from second-heaven warfare, and exhausted from circling around the same path and declare, "THIS IS THE WAY FORWARD! THIS IS THE WAY OUT OF JEZEBEL FOREST."

He's washing many with the pure water of His Word. Washing off those false words that claimed to be from Him! Those sticky spiderweb words that didn't reflect His heart and tried to control your anointing and keep you stuck in seasons you outgrew. They are blowing like ash in the wind. Swept away under tidal waves of truth and grace. They no longer define you because they never *did* define you. Man can't redefine what heaven has already defined.

This feels like a significant day for restoration and rebuilding. He's restoring more than you lost. He's stretching your tent pegs wider. He's unyoking you from wrong systems, situations, and agendas and yoking you to the kingdom alignments He has established for the future He's prepared for you. He's expanded your capacity in secret while you rest in the secret place. He's been increasing your territory when you weren't looking. He's been flawlessly leading you into the land you're called to occupy. I feel the Lord declaring over YOU today, "BREATHE THE FRESH AIR AGAIN, and receive the double portion of My recompense, pleasure, and permission over you." Because God said:

> "I will give him the key to the house of David—the highest position in the royal court. When he opens doors, no one will be able to close them; when he closes doors, no one will be able to open them." —Isaiah 22:22 (NLT)

If you've been in a long, weary, painful, and confusing season of unexpected blows from hell targeted again and again at your identity and calling, THIS IS YOUR DAY TO BREATHE

AGAIN! Stop allowing those curses to cut you. Stop allowing yourself to get sucked up into battles you weren't called to fight and into woodchippers heaven didn't throw you in. Stop focusing on what the enemy has done, and refocus your gaze on what heaven IS doing right now.

It's time to step out of the cave of silence you were chased into and remember who He created you to be. Don't tiptoe fearfully out of the cave, looking over your shoulder suspiciously, wondering how long it will take before the next rejection, squinting at the brightness of the sun because it's felt dark for so long. Bust out of that cave, and step into the bright light of a new day with the joy of the Lord in every confident step you take and every new relationship you build. No more looking at the past with regret.

It's a brand new day in a brave new world.

IT'S A BRAND NEW DAY IN A BRAVE NEW WORLD.

For too long, you've conformed to what you thought would be safe. You've allowed accusations from hell a seat at your table. But no more! All those lies are exposed and evicted today, and they are found hollow and fruitless. WE BREAK EVERY SOUL TIE AND EVERY AGREEMENT WITH EACH AND EVERY LIE. It's time to release the unique sound of heaven that's been locked away. It's time to plow through the fear of man and bring your oil to the feet of Jesus. This is the season you pour it all, and you don't walk on eggshells tiptoeing around trying to please man. You're going to step back into every promise you were chased out of with your discernment and love intact—no longer jaded and isolated by the wounds of the last season, and it won't be through rebellion or striving. The Lord Himself will delight in opening these doors for you because "He reveals deep and hidden things; he knows what lies in darkness, and light dwells with him" (Daniel 2:22, NIV).

There is a unique and powerful anointing resting on your life that God created ONLY you to release on the earth. Nobody can do it exactly like you can. So shake off the dust of what was lost, and step into joyful obedience and bridal expectation! The Bridegroom is coming, and we don't need more revival or bridal language; we need BRIDAL INTIMACY.

The enemy knows how to use people to discourage you and distract you from your calling. There will always be pushback and resistance because what you carry is valuable. There will always be warfare this side of heaven. There will always be naysayers around your destiny. Your obedience doesn't require people's understanding. It's time to come higher and walk in truth.

Imagine a doctor giving a healthy person a diagnosis of an infectious disease. No matter how healthy they are, the doctor keeps this patient in isolation, stands by his wrong diagnosis, and rejects all the evidence to the contrary. A more experienced doctor comes in and calls the patient clean, but the doctor will not change his diagnosis. That doctor would probably lose his license and probably go to prison for abuse and malpractice. At best, it's because of a lack of knowledge:

"Our present knowledge and our prophecies are but partial" (1 Corinthians 13:9, TPT).

Sometimes in the church, we misdiagnose people, and call it discernment. It causes more bondage than the patient walked in with. We all make mistakes, but when we're unable to receive correction about those mistakes and claim infallibility, it's a lot like malpractice. It doesn't care what the Great Physician says about a person's health, what the Bible says, or the actual facts. Accusation has a diagnosis from hell claiming it's from heaven, and it is unable to change the report because it's unable to admit error. That's how you know a discernment ministry has turned into an accusation ministry. You can *say* it's helpful and loving, but to the receiver, it feels a lot like a woodchipper. Love is the hinge on the door of every prophetic gift. His love flowing through us creates pathways for us to hear more clearly.

We need the same love:

> Anyone can say, "I love God," yet have hatred toward another believer. This makes him a phony because if you don't love a brother or sister, whom you can see, how can you truly love God, whom you can't see? For he has given us this command: whoever loves God must also demonstrate love to others."
> —1 John 4:20-21 (TPT)

If you're only expressing the demons and dysfunctions you see in other believers and not the purposes of heaven over them, your discernment is immature, and you're going to crush a lot of people. We should *especially* be gentle with those we're correcting or discerning things about. Excessive punishment leads to excessive sorrow. We can't love people and also make them drown in our rejection. Follow 2 Corinthians 2:6-8 (TPT):

> I believe that your united rebuke has been punishment enough for him. Instead of more punishment, what he needs most is your encouragement through your gracious display of forgiveness. I beg you to reaffirm your deep love for him.

If there's more *FOR* us than against us (meaning we have more angel help than demon opposition), then what does it mean when we only see demons working in people/situations? It means something is off with our vision. Testing spirits means discerning how God is working things together for *good* too. Let's not be ignorant about the activity of hell, but also let's not glorify it above Jesus. If the enemy consumes our focus or conversations more than Jesus, we're being set up.

I touched on this earlier, but healthy houses don't try to disciple demons, and they don't try to cast out the flesh. If you confuse the two, you won't have time to equip the church because you'll be in constant damage-control mode. Next to a church that doesn't act like they even *have* an enemy, I haven't seen many things do as much damage as believers with a hyperfocus on the activity of demons and believers who refuse to receive correction for error because of jealousy, pride, and rebellion.

If we can't be teachable, the Bible says we aren't true sons:

> We all should welcome God's discipline as the validation of authentic sonship. For if we have never once

endured his correction it only proves we are strangers and not sons. —Hebrews 12:8 (TPT)

Translated in the Greek, it means we're illegitimate. The King James Version calls children who don't get corrected by God "bastards." So if we have a problem with being fathered by God, we're manifesting our true condition as orphans. Orphans don't know how to receive a father or mother's correction. They think everything is an attack.

Biblical discernment is aligned with hope and redemption and is able to give *and* receive correction. When I see people, I am now very conscious of what heaven sees in them, but my thoughts alone don't push back hell. My prayers do, so I open my mouth, speak the beauty I see, and bind the works of darkness trying to interfere with that person's destiny. All of us who help walk others into freedom need to protect the purity of that holy calling.

BIBLICAL DISCERNMENT IS ALIGNED WITH HOPE AND REDEMPTION AND IS ABLE TO GIVE AND RECEIVE CORRECTION.

What is more honest than God's heart? Certainly not a person's choices, struggles, or strongholds. We have to honor the gift of heaven on the inside without tripping over who they're not on the outside. It's taken decades to cultivate this in my own life, and I'm *still* learning. It's a perversion of the gospel to say God told you to reject people and that the activity of hell in their life is more powerful than the purposes of heaven to redeem them. There are lost people but no unredeemable ones. It grieves Jesus when we misrepresent His heart and underestimate His blood.

His blood speaks a better word over people. Calling people up to how heaven sees them is always more effective than demonizing them. People come alive when they know God's heart. There is deliverance in partnering with the truth of heaven. Let's pick the kingdom and call the people around us up into their new identity in Christ.

We've practiced this forever with our kids from before their birth. The fruit is good! Even their names speak to their purpose. When I tell my kids I trust them, guess what happens? They behave even more trustworthy. If I were to tell my kids I can't trust them, guess what would happen—the opposite of what I want to happen. They would lower their standards to match my expectations of them. If I say, "You never listen," well, I just cursed my kids to never listen. Awesome.

Words are SERIOUS. It's why we never said terrible twos or cursed their teen years by saying, "If you think it's bad now, just wait until they're teenagers." Nope. You don't have to speak or receive a curse from hell over your children, yourself, or anyone else. We choose to speak blessings over *all* their years. We always said terrific twos and teens, and we're still living in the sweet fruit of that harvest because words are powerful enough to break curses or make them. It is not delusional to believe the best and see the gold; it is prophetic.

Offense and judgment cannot see people clearly. True discernment requires a foundation of deep humility and love.

It requires a heart like David's in Psalm 139:23 (author paraphrase), "Search me. Know me. Test me. Reveal offense." The proof will always be in the fruit. One gives life and leads people to deep wells of the Father's heart. It's gentle and kind. The other destroys, wounds, divides, and cancels. We have to stop demonizing people and start fighting the right enemy.

Standing as a judge over someone else's hidden motives is one of the most out-of-line with Scripture activities a believer can participate in:

> After all, who can really see into a person's heart and know his hidden impulses except for that person's spirit? So it is with God. His thoughts and secrets are only fully understood by his Spirit, the Spirit of God."
> —1 Corinthians 2:11 (TPT)

Knowing our own heart is impossible. How can we possibly know someone else's? Offense kills discernment. It causes us to elevate and often misdiagnose demonic activity. It blinds us, and we bring people destruction instead of freedom. Confusion instead of clarity. If you've caused damage and pain, haven't we all, there's no condemnation. Just a plea to clean up the messes you can and behave.

Most slander is rooted in jealousy:

> But when some of the Jews saw the crowds, they were jealous; so they slandered Paul and argued against whatever he said." —Acts 13:45 (NLT)

When people's identities aren't rooted deeply in Jesus, they have to discredit others to feel better about themselves. But good news: Jesus doesn't listen to slander, and He doesn't partner with accusers. He exposes the fruit for what it is. You want to overcome jealousy? Do the opposite of what Satan is telling you to do. The cure for any and all jealousy the enemy tries to entangle you in is always honor. Show honor in the very place you feel the sting of comparison. Go above and beyond. Your heart will follow your mouth out of darkness and into light.

An orphan mentality strives to be heard and seen and to find significance in the approval and validation of others. It looks for opportunities to discredit the significance of others in an effort to validate their own need for worth. It doesn't understand the Father's heart. Sons and daughters know they are welcome at the table, and there's plenty of room for everyone.

Celebrating the gift, success, favor, and anointing of others comes naturally when your identity is rooted in the absolute pleasure of a good God. You wanna kill the jealousy, striving, and fighting for position and rank in your life that's robbing you of joy? Go low, and stay low. Be the crazy person cheering people on and calling out the best in others in an ocean full of critics and naysayers. Honor confuses hell. Demons don't know how to attack a grateful and honoring believer.

HONOR CONFUSES HELL. DEMONS DON'T KNOW HOW TO ATTACK A GRATEFUL AND HONORING BELIEVER.

Don't be the person known for seeing the worst in everything. It's really just insecurity and self-doubt. There is enough room at the table for you. Celebrating the gifts, success, favor, and anointing on someone else kills jealousy. Comparison leaves you in a constant struggle for joy. The joy of the Lord is our strength. Comparison drains our strength. It places our eyes on our lack instead of the reality that we lack nothing in Christ. I like what God told my oldest son, Josiah, about comparison: *Don't compare. Come.* Come to the table. Come back to your First Love. Get a fresh revelation of God's heart. Worshipful gratitude kills comparison.

Honor changes culture. It deadens jealousy, rivalry, and disunity. It pours water on the fires of slander, gossip, and rejection. It evicts territorial spirits from regions. Honor cancels confusion and gives the parts that have less honor double. It rescues people from the grief of punishment. It pulls outsiders in and loves them into wholeness just to send them out again to transform culture.

If you're struggling with jealousy, put down the stones of accusation and promote that person above yourself. Champion them in their calling. Ask the Lord to show you what about them is lacking in your life. Don't put your mouth against God's image bearers. Support them. Serve them. Bless them. Doors have a way of opening faster for you when you posture yourself in humility and hold them open for others. Honor brings heaven to earth and the kingdom to the church. Above all: "Let gentleness be seen in every relationship, for our Lord is ever near" (Philippians 4:5, TPT).

If you've walked through the pain of being rejected and misunderstood, the Lord is speaking over your heart:

UNCANCELED. People can throw your relationship in a woodchipper, but they can never throw you or your calling in there. All of those sticky spiderweb labels and accusations slide right off of you. Man can't define your value because Jesus already has, according to Isaiah 54:17 (NLT):

> In that coming day no weapon turned against you will succeed. You will silence every voice raised up to accuse you. These benefits are enjoyed by the servants of the Lord; their vindication will come from me. I, the Lord, have spoken!

Sin and compromise can forfeit assignments and delay the promise. They're death wrapped in pleasure because we chose to die to our flesh in installments instead of just dying fully to the old man. The very nature of sin is that it will always cost more than you bargained for. We can choose our sin, but we can't pick our consequences. Some of you may be living out the consequences of some costly choices you've made. God is not finished. Your story is not over! There are no unredeemable situations or people. None of us has the power to decide who goes in the woodchipper.

When we confess our sins He is faithful and just to forgive them. But consequences may still be in motion:

> The harvest you reap reveals the seed that you planted. If you plant the corrupt seeds of self-life into this natural realm, you can expect a harvest of corruption. If you plant the good seeds of Spirit-life you will reap beautiful fruits that grow from the everlasting life of the Spirit." Galatians 6:8 (TPT)

If you're in that season, know that heaven doesn't speak a language of hopelessness. There is no more condemnation for those who belong to Christ. He calls you CLEAN. You have permission to become more like Jesus. We're ALL growing up into the fullness of Christ. People may have experienced YOU 1.0, but that failure, trauma, or immaturity doesn't disqualify you from picking up things you mishandled in one season and stewarding them excellently in the next because "The godly may trip 7 times, but they will get up again" (Proverbs 24:16, NLT). Keep getting up!

PEOPLE MAY HAVE EXPERIENCED YOU 1.0, BUT THAT FAILURE, TRAUMA, OR IMMATURITY DOESN'T DISQUALIFY YOU FROM PICKING UP THINGS YOU MISHANDLED IN ONE SEASON AND STEWARDING THEM EXCELLENTLY IN THE NEXT.

HOW TO MOVE FORWARD AFTER FAILURE:
- » Confess your sins and ask for forgiveness.
- » Accept the consequences.
- » Set up boundaries to prevent repeated failure.
- » Bear fruit in keeping with repentance. Words of repentance are not the same as fruit of repentance. It's changed behavior over time. John the Baptist said, "Prove by how you live that you've repented." (Matthew 3:8, MSG)
- » Give yourself grace even if others won't.

- » Humility is the way forward.
- » Don't make excuses or shift blame.
- » Clean up messes where you can.
- » Align with what heaven is saying over you.
- » Align your mindsets and beliefs to reflect Scripture.

Sometimes, man's rejection is the protection of the Lord. He is creating space to prune, cut back, and upgrade the fruitfulness of your life. Don't confuse pruning with correction. Sometimes, it's not a sign you've done something wrong. Often, it's a sign you've done many things right. Pruning is a reward for being faithful and fruitful. The following verses prove this:

- » "He cuts off every branch of mine that doesn't produce fruit, and he prunes the branches that do bear fruit so they will produce even more." —John 15:2 (NLT)
- » "Remain in me, and I will remain in you. For a branch cannot produce fruit if it is severed from the vine, and you cannot be fruitful unless you remain in me." —John 15:4 (NLT)

Read what Paul said to Timothy, do what he says, and be prepared:

> So Timothy, my son, I am entrusting you with this responsibility, in keeping with the very first prophecies that were spoken over your life, and are now in the process of fulfillment in this great work of ministry, in keeping with the prophecies spoken over you. With this encouragement use your prophecies as weapons as you wage spiritual warfare by faith

and with a clean conscience. For there are many who reject these virtues and are now destitute of the true faith. — 1 Timothy 1:18-19 (TPT)

PIONEER PRAYER:

Father, thank You that You've written redemption into every part of my story. Thank You that you speak a better word over my life than the accuser. I choose to align my mind with every word You speak over my future and identity. I choose to extend that same mercy to others that I've been given. Clean the filters of my discernment. Thank You that man can't cancel what You've established in my life. Thank You that nothing can throw me in the woodchipper or separate me from Your love. In Jesus's Name. Amen.

Pioneer Prompt:

Like Paul instructed Timothy, war with the prophetic words spoken over your life. Write down promises God has spoken directly through His Word to you. Create a library of personalized prophetic weapons to use when the enemy comes in with arrows of accusation. Feast on every word the Father is speaking over your identity. Journal His response, and if you're struggling with offense or the enemy has been trying to recruit you to be on his accusation committee, listen to God's voice over your enemies. What does He love about them? What do they carry that He values? Seeing people after the Spirit instead of the flesh is the most kingdom thing we can do. Bless and do not curse. This will not be easy but kingdom pioneers are not called to take the easy path. Journal what the Lord reveals.

_____
_____
_____
_____
_____
_____
_____
_____

CHAPTER 6

The Priesthood

In the early 2000s, a prophet from South Africa came to speak at our church. It was toward the end of his ministry time, and I honestly wasn't expecting a word at this point. But he called me out of the crowd, and I was ready for it. "Prophetess to the nations," or something similarly validating would have been amazing. Ha-ha! But that was not the word I received. Instead, he pointed at me and said, with a thick, intimidating accent, "You are not qualified" (insert pause for dramatic effect), "but you are called, and your calling will take you places your qualifications never could."

Jesus only has one kind of people. Your church only has one kind of people. Your family has only one kind of people: CALLED people. You may not feel very qualified, but called trumps qualified all day, every day of the week. Your calling will make space for you. Your calling will open unusual doors and opportunities. There is an invisible grace operating at all times, enabling you to walk faithfully in this unique calling.

This has been the witness of my life:

> But God chose those whom the world considers foolish to shame those who think they are wise, and God chose the puny and powerless to shame the high and mighty. He chose the lowly, the laughable in the world's eyes—nobodies—so that he would shame the somebodies. For he chose what is regarded as insignificant in order to supersede what is regarded as prominent, so that there would be no place for prideful boasting in God's presence."
> —1 Corinthians 1:27-29 (TPT)

I have experienced such unusual grace and unmerited favor, and I haven't had to self-promote, climb a ladder, network my way up, or pry open one single door to make things happen through my own effort. God doesn't just train His servants in classrooms. Oftentimes, He trains them on the backside of a wilderness for forty years. A lot of what I've learned in a classroom I've had to unlearn—while the wilderness lessons have stuck.

A LOT OF WHAT I'VE LEARNED IN A CLASSROOM I'VE HAD TO UNLEARN—WHILE THE WILDERNESS LESSONS HAVE STUCK.

God made it very clear He would be the only builder of any ministry flowing out of my life. I've never applied for a single ministry position, but for the last twenty years, in His timing, the right door has always opened. I haven't had to know the right people, yet God would always bring those alignments in and out of different seasons. Maybe your journey has looked completely different from mine. Regardless of how the doors open, favor always works better than striving to be seen. When you stay faithful, God notices. I've stayed faithful in hidden fields of preparation and in the little things, and God sent Samuel with some oil to come find me. God knows how to speak to your Samuel, and the Lord has given him specific instructions:

> Do not consider his appearance or his height, for I have rejected him. The Lord does not look at the things people look at. People look at the outward appearance, but the Lord looks at the heart."
> —1 Samuel 16:7 (NIV)

Obscurity is not punishment. It's preparation.

If you are a follower of Christ, then you are a minister. Congratulations! Welcome to the priesthood of ALL believers. You might not have a microphone, a stage, or a title before your name, but you are a minister ordained by King Jesus Himself. The Great Commission is YOUR mission. You don't need Elijah to throw his cloak around your shoulders; Jesus has directly commissioned you.

I have served just about everywhere a person can serve in a church: janitor, pastor, worship leader, youth, kids church, counselor, office administration, social media, graphic design, Bible teacher, greeter, outreach director, app and website design, photographer, and creative director. Maybe you can relate. I'm pretty sure I'm leaving some things out, but this is what I've learned: not serving in an area because it's not your "gifting" reeks of entitlement. Look at Peter and Paul. An uneducated fisherman and a religious scholar who had been a Pharisee of Pharisees. If they were alive today we would give them a spiritual gifts test and definitely conclude that Paul should be an apostle to the Jews and Peter to the gentiles. But God flips the script and uses them both powerfully in unexpected ways. Peter to the Jews and Paul to the gentiles. Our weakness is often exactly the right container for His glory to be revealed. If you can't steward a mop, you're not ready for a microphone. Sometimes, it's better to sit at the altar with Jesus until He's the one thing your heart desires most. If it's a struggle, it's probably a good indication your craving for a platform has superseded your need for an altar.

Maybe you're not about the stage at all, but God's called you to be a voice in the kingdom, and your comfort and the fear of man are keeping you from stepping out in obedience. Performance anxiety is the flesh. There is freedom when we start measuring success and maturity by the response time of our obedience instead of the results we can measure. Who are we to tell God how He can use us? We don't pick our gifts out of a Sears catalog. (Is that still a thing, or am I dating myself?) Who are we to deny Jesus what He asks for? Can you even imagine if Noah told God he couldn't build the ark because craftsmanship was his bottom gift? Maybe Paul was more qualified to preach to Jews but he wasn't called. Peter was. God's calling qualifies you too.

Entitlement wants a harvest it didn't sow. It wants glory without suffering. It wants gifts to display without sacrifice or serving. Gifts are 100 percent about serving—not about positions on a team. I've found that God will oftentimes put me in positions that are *not* my gifting to mature me. My top gifts are prophesy, exhortation, discernment, and wisdom. Guess what my bottom gift is: administration—right next to craftsmanship. Guess how the Lord has helped me kill my flesh? Bingo. Teaching me how to serve and stay faithful from my weaknesses. My roots have gotten deeper, my dependency on Jesus has gotten stronger, my fruit has gotten sweeter, and my pride has gotten deader. It's actually, somehow, made the gifts I supernaturally already operate in even more clear and versatile. That's what happens when you say yes to yieldedness and not merely giftedness. Your tent expands. Your capacity to carry more oil expands. Your territory expands. And ultimately, your love expands.

Your gifts will often make space for you around really significant tables. Sometimes, the agendas of man will try to yoke themselves to your gift with self-serving interest. If you steward your gifts well, there is never a shortage of balls to juggle and opportunities to say yes to. The reward for faithfulness is more to steward. But you only have *one* family. One marriage. Everything you say yes to is something else you have to say no to, so make sure you're saying yes to the things that hold eternal value and not just the things that give you temporary validation.

There's an invisible warning label attached to your gift. It reads something like this:

Warning! Powerful gifts operating here. Handle with care. Just because they can, doesn't mean they should. Overuse will diminish their shelf life. Some side effects of possible malfunction may include thinking they are irreplaceable and that the church cannot function without them. Doing things robotically instead of from delight. Feeling an overwhelming sense of pride that without them, nothing will get done right. Burnout from poor boundaries. Depending heavily on their own performance. If unplugged from their power source, they will cause harm to themselves and others. Ask them how they're doing, and don't accept a fake answer.

People will take what you give them. But only you and Jesus know your own capacity, and it changes in every season. So open your mouth, and kindly communicate your boundaries. Just the other day, someone asked me to help them with a ministry project. I so badly wanted to say yes. I'm good with saying no over text, but when you catch me face to face, those old people-pleasing habits die hard. Ha-ha! Thankfully, I was self-aware enough to recognize my capacity was too limited to say yes. They pushed a little more. So, I politely but more firmly said, "I'm sorry. I want to say yes, but I do not have the capacity right now to help you, and if I tried to push beyond my capacity, I wouldn't be much good to anyone." They received my no beautifully, and we all survived.

OUR CAPACITY IS LIKE A HOUSE OF CARDS. ONE CARD BY ITSELF ISN'T MUCH, BUT IF YOU PLACE THAT CARD AT THE TOP OF YOUR ALREADY COMPLETE STRUCTURE, IT CAN CAUSE THE WHOLE HOUSE TO COLLAPSE.

Our capacity is like a house of cards. One card by itself isn't much, but if you place that card at the top of your already complete structure, it can cause the whole house to collapse. From the outside looking in, people may think you're pretty weak: *It's just one tiny card.* But they don't know about all the other cards. So we can never assume or pass judgment on other people's capacity. Safe people who love you will protect your boundaries and honor your capacity. Only people who are using you will be upset.

Wanting to quit could be an indicator that you've been pushing your capacity for too long. If you feel like quitting, maybe it's time to rest and reevaluate things. Maybe you're still carrying things from a former season that Jesus didn't ask you to continue carrying into this new season. There are seasons when I need to shake off the excess and let the ministry flowing through my life get really simple. Those seasons always make space for increased capacity in the next season, and I've found that in the seasons I didn't honor my capacity, it has shrunk before I stepped into the next one.

Not stewarding your gifts well can also impact future opportunities. If you're waiting for a title to use them, you may be waiting for a long time. A title and a platform may expand your influence, but they don't give your gifts more value or relevance. I can prophesy and exhort around the dinner table. I can dream dreams and hear God's heart while I'm not even awake. I can equip my sons in our home. I can speak life into my marriage. Is it less significant because it's outside the structure of a church building? Is it less significant because it's ministry only Jesus and my inner circle see? Or maybe is it the main pathway God intended gifts to be used—in our ordinary everyday living and not just Sundays in a building?

When I was a young Bible student, I went to an apostolic conference to serve. It was kind of like being a fly on a wall. I was there to *serve,* but I was also receiving a ton of impartation and ministry. A prophet laid hands on me and said I'm like John the Baptist, and I fell backward under the power of the Holy Spirit. You have to understand. I grew up Catholic. Then I was Baptist for many years after that. Falling out under the power of God wasn't part of my denominational upbringing. This is the part where I encourage you not to check out on me because you may disagree with me doctrinally. I'm sure there's a lot more that connects us than separates us. There's a point in sharing these experiences. As a teenager, I was alone in my house one night and happened to turn on a program by a guy named Benny Hinn I had never heard of before. Before I even knew what hit me, I was baptized in the Holy Spirit and speaking in tongues. I had never heard tongues and didn't even know what it was or why it was happening, but the power of God filled the whole house, and I could barely walk under the weight of it.

So, back to my story. I was at this apostolic conference. I got hit by the power of God, made my way back to my seat, and all of the sudden, I started hearing a word for an older Indian lady who was at the altar praying. I was young. I was in a different church, in a different state. I didn't know anybody—who they were or why they were there. Nothing. But I couldn't shake the word God kept telling me to share with this stranger. Finally, I mustered up enough courage and innocently went to talk to her. As I walked to the front, the enemy was making me super aware of how unspiritual and simple the word sounded. But what's the worst that could happen? She would probably smile, nod, say thank you, and the exchange would be over. So I leaned over to the lady and said, "You don't know me. But God wanted me to come tell you that He is taking you higher."

The lady burst into tears under the power of God. It was such an intense moment; the service shifted and became ministry to this lady. She was weeping. Apostles and prophets gathered around her, and I just stood there in the middle of it feeling really out of my element. They asked me to lay hands on her and pray, so I did, and she began to share her testimony about how she and her husband were missionaries to India. Ministry had gotten very hard. They were weary and came to the conference hoping to discern if God's will was to stay in the states or continue their work in India. She had told the Lord, "If someone comes up to me and tells me you are taking me higher, then I will know you are calling us to stay on the mission field."

And that was the defining moment when I realized God *only* needs our obedience. Our tiny simple containers are enough. They left that conference with a clear confirmation from the

Lord and fresh wind in their sails. I'll never see the fruit that came from that encounter this side of heaven. I don't even know who they were. But my simple, unimpressive obedience was enough in the hands of a very capable God, and so is yours. And this is the beauty of the body and how we use our gifts to serve one another.

MY SIMPLE, UNIMPRESSIVE OBEDIENCE WAS ENOUGH IN THE HANDS OF A VERY CAPABLE GOD, AND SO IS YOURS.

But what if I had tried to make the word sound impressive by speaking more into it than God told me to? "I am going to use your life to transform nations, and you shall ascend the hill of the Lord, and the power of God will rest upon you—thus saith the Lord." That would have made *me* look more spiritual, but it wouldn't have served *her* or delivered to her the time-sensitive confirmation she requested from the Lord. The Lord taught me early on not to add or take away from anything He was speaking. If it's one word, that's all I'm speaking. If it's one prophetic act and no explanation at all, that's what I'm doing.

Anytime a word is funneled down through a person, there's going to be some of *us* that get mixed into the word. However, as much as possible, I want to be someone He can trust not to mix my ego and agendas into the delivery of His heart to people. We don't have to make our gifts look more impressive than they are; we just have to focus on simple obedience.

Obedience is the love language of heaven. Obedience is our job, results belong to the Lord.

A gift operating in our life isn't our time to shine. It's our time to *serve* and to partner with God's heart for people. Let me be really honest with you guys; maybe this is an area I haven't fully died to myself, but when I see people performing in their ministry to look and sound impressive, DEFCON 1 is going off in my spirit. Every alarm is ringing. Mostly because I love that person and want to see Jesus bring them freedom, but it's also just a struggle coming into agreement with a performer. I take agreement seriously. If I'm going to yoke my yes to your amen, I want to make sure the ministry flowing isn't marked with self-promotion. We obviously can't judge the heart, but there are signs when performance is operating in a believer or ministry. I know because I've been one. If any of these resonate, you may be operating as a performer instead of a priest, and Jesus wants to bring you freedom. And to the pastor reading this, discipleship has to be the greater value in your church.

SIGNS OF A PERFORMANCE MENTALITY:

- » They mimic other people's oil and take credit for it.
- » They always bring the same level of intensity to every gathering, even if it pulls you in the opposite direction from where the Spirit was leading.
- » They struggle to follow the Spirit because that's not the direction the crowd wants to go.
- » They get performance anxiety. (This is the flesh.)
- » They are overcautious of the opinions of people.
- » They pull the room's focus away from Jesus.

- » They have attention-seeking tendencies—yet will do anything to avoid negative attention.
- » They have a script for everything.
- » They overthink and over plan.
- » They struggle with authenticity.

Your journey with Jesus didn't start with doing and performing. It started with receiving and being, and it ends the same way it began. We aren't promoted into performance the further along we get up the ministry ladder. It's actually a departure from sonship. Performing is easy. Discipleship is costly. God wants to align our ecclesiology (biblical view of the church) back to His original heart and design. If you are a full-time saint, then you are in full-time ministry. You trade the performance hat for priestly garments. It's more than two hours on a Sunday; it's a lifestyle of yielding to Jesus. We love Him by serving what He loves. Jesus loves the bride. Being a kingdom pioneer means returning to His original design for how gifts operate in the church.

To move in governmental equipping offices in the body, it's important that you aren't a self-appointed lone ranger but called and anointed by God, biblically qualified, and affirmed to operate in that office by other church leadership. You can be prophetic but not operate in the office of a prophet. Acts tells us in the last days He'll pour out His Spirit on ALL flesh, and sons and daughters will *prophesy*. You can be a pastor and not operate in the office of a shepherd. If you're a parent, you're called to be the most influential pastor in your child's life. This is a kingdom of *priests* not of titles. For every other gift given to the church that isn't one of the Five-Fold governmental offices you get to decide who called you—God or man:

> But you are the ones chosen by God, chosen for the high calling of priestly work, chosen to be a holy people, God's instruments to do his work and speak out for him, to tell others of the night-and-day difference he made for you—from nothing to something, from rejected to accepted. —Peter 2:9-10 (TPT)

It might not be your vocational calling, but ministering to Jesus and His bride is your full-time assignment. Wherever your feet step, that's your mission field. We cannot hold onto our forms and onto Jesus at the same time. We cannot hide behind our titles and think we're living out the Great Commission.

IT MIGHT NOT BE YOUR VOCATIONAL CALLING, BUT MINISTERING TO JESUS AND HIS BRIDE IS YOUR FULL-TIME ASSIGNMENT.

People are dying. We need to break off the fear of man and be fully awakened to God's love. Our gifts and positions are for serving and edifying. Tools to reach the lost. Tools to strengthen the bride. Not about us whatsoever. People can flaunt their gifts on earth like badges of honor and still be locked out of their own wedding. Gifts are good for nothing if we're not using them to point people to Jesus.

In 2020, our city shut down, and we started gathering friends and neighbors in our home for church. A few months later, that ended up being the new model for the whole church. Not because of a global pandemic, but because prior to that the Lord had already been releasing a vision to our pastor of the church gathering in homes and campuses all over the nation. It's always nice when the Lord gives you a heads up because oftentimes He doesn't. If you want to know what threatens the enemy, it's people moving out of old wineskins. But we've found the new wineskin is really the original wineskin. It's family. It's the book of Acts. The tip of his spear is pointed at family. It's pointed at pioneers returning to the things that truly matter to His heart. Family is at the helm of this reformation.

But it would be very hypocritical to think a venue change or a full altar is reformation. True reformation usually comes with deep costs and resistance that leads to lasting heart transformation. True reformation is a returning to the things that have always mattered to the heart of the Father. The sad truth is there is idolatry in the church that makes it very hard for the Lord to interrupt our system with His presence. And His presence is truly the one and only thing we need.

We are not called to worship models or methods. Both models and methods change. But gathering with the church in our home and seeing things we only read about in Acts happening inside our home, was truly the reset we needed to break free from some consumer mindsets that were driving a lot of our ministry.

I get that what I'm saying isn't popular because others are speaking a different narrative that sounds like, "We can't be the church from our couch, watching a screen in a living room." But hearing different perspectives can actually be really healthy and protect you from standing in an echo chamber. Not everyone was chased into their homes because of fear. Some were invited to return to the simplicity of home to host revival and break bread around tables. I'd propose that if you can't be the church gathered with neighbors in your home, you're probably going to struggle to be the church anywhere. You may also struggle to explain the entire book of Acts and the birth of the church.

It's not our job to judge other models; it's our job to obey the assignments we've been given. We have friends in megachurches seeing real revival and substance. We have friends who gather in fields for church, and the presence of God is beautifully working and transforming hearts there too. Wherever Jesus is, that's where revival can happen and that's where I want to be. Instead of slandering it and getting hung up on preferences, we *could be* celebrating the Great Commission and the creativity of a limitless God and church. Sometimes we place value on things heaven never did, and we go to war with people to cling onto those things when we're really resisting the river of God wanting to transform our cities. He isn't obligated to sustain moves He didn't start. And He isn't obligated to explain Himself when He starts a move you didn't see coming.

Methods are constantly changing. It's a flowing river. The message *doesn't* change. Jesus is the only Builder. He's the same yesterday, today, and forever. His Word is eternal. Let's let Him build churches that are attractive to HIM and not get hung up on our traditions and preferences. He is doing something new *on purpose*. Breaking you out of the box and leading you through a wilderness way you haven't been before. Honor previous seasons (they served a purpose), feast on His faithfulness, but if He's calling you to something new I'd encourage you to obey even if it costs you everything and nobody understands it. Don't suppress the fullest measure of what God is wanting to release through you. Don't wait for man's permission. We want to shepherd people through transition gently and carefully, but our obedience should never hinge on their permission.

> So if you're serious about living this new resurrection life with Christ, act like it. Pursue the things over which Christ presides. Don't shuffle along, eyes to the ground, absorbed with the things right in front of you. Look up, and be alert to what is going on around Christ—that's where the action is. See things from his perspective. Your old life is dead. Your new life, which is your real life—even though invisible to spectators—is with Christ in God. He is your life. When Christ (your real life, remember) shows up again on this earth, you'll show up, too—the real you, the glorious you. Meanwhile, be content with obscurity, like Christ. —Colossians 3:1-4 (MSG)

There is a Grand Canyon-sized gap we have a very challenging time reconciling, between what we read in Acts and the Epistles and the church models of today. The New Testament Ecclesia was in no way created to be a consumer-driven organization. It was a living organism full of contributors. We've relegated church to be an event we attend instead of a body we belong to.

I heard somewhere that something like 98 percent of Christians aren't in full-time vocational ministry. Maybe that's outdated by the time you read this, but it would appear to be accurate if you look in our churches at the ratio of staff to attendees. God did not create this model. There is no way 2 percent of the body of Christ can carry the advancement of the kingdom on their backs. It's going to take a long, long, long time to bring in the harvest that way. What does Jesus have to say about the harvest?

> "The harvest is great, but the workers are few. So pray to the Lord who is in charge of the harvest; ask him to send more workers into his fields. Now go, and remember that I am sending you out as lambs among wolves." —Luke 10:2 (NLT)

Clearly, Jesus recognized that the worker-to-harvest ratio was out of balance. But He didn't stop short at noticing the workers were few. That's usually where we stop. He went on to command us to PRAY for God to send more workers. You and I stepping into the fullness of our callings was a dream in the heart of Jesus thousands of years before we ever were born. Lou Engle describes it this way: " You think you have a dream, but you don't have a dream. God had a dream and wrapped your flesh around it."

In the Old Testament, only about 10 percent of the people were called to be priests. One-tenth of the people were called by God to be in full-time vocational ministry. The birth of the church was not the end of the priesthood. It was the greater realization of it. Israel was delivered through the blood of a

Passover Lamb. Jesus became our Passover Lamb, and His blood fulfilled it all to include us in this priesthood: "He has made us a Kingdom of priests for God his Father. All glory and power to him forever and ever! Amen" (Revelation 1:6, NLT).

There's another interesting verse in Revelation 2:6 (author paraphrase) where Jesus says, "Although to your credit, you despise the practices of the Nicolaitans, which I also despise." One of the reasons Jesus hates the deeds of this group called the Nicolaitans was because historically they were full of compromise and didn't recognize the priesthood of all believers. Instead, they created separations in the church between clergy and laypeople to conquer and rule over the people.

Because of this ancient spirit of religious control and self-promotion, many believers struggle to realize that the Great Commission is THEIR mission too. One day you're going to stand before God and give an account for how you stewarded your time on this earth. "I paid the pastor to do it" won't pass for an excuse. Why?

> "All authority in heaven and on earth has been given to me. Go therefore and make disciples of all nations, baptizing them in the name of the Father and of the Son and of the Holy Spirit, teaching them to observe all that I have commanded you. And behold, I am with you always, to the end of the age."
> —Matthew 28:18-20 (ESV)

I grew up on a large poultry farm. We raised about fifty thousand turkeys at a time. We didn't have hired help. It was just my parents and us. Farming is hard labor. I would go to basketball practice with bloody blistered hands, but it didn't feel like hard labor. It felt like what it meant to be a part of a family. Everyone together pitching in and enjoying the fruit of our hard work. This is an all-hands-on-the-plow era for the daughters and sons of God: "Anyone who puts a hand to the plow and then looks back is not fit for the Kingdom of God" Luke 9:62 (NLT), and "All who are obsessed with being secure in life will lose it all—including their lives. But those who let go of their lives and surrender them to me will discover true life." Luke 17:33 (TPT)

THIS IS A BEAUTIFUL REALITY. GOD WILL NEVER USE YOU TO ABUSE YOU. YOU'RE NOT SOME TOOL IN HIS TOOL BELT HE ONLY PULLS OUT TO USE.

And here is a beautiful reality. God will never use you to abuse you. You're not some tool in His tool belt He only pulls out to use. Orphans agree to things for acceptance. We are not orphans. We are fully accepted sons and daughters, and the kingdom is ALL about partnership with the Spirit. We don't get close to the Father through striving to be pure enough. It's through Jesus and Jesus alone. Two thousand years from now it will still be through the person of Jesus. Even when the world is screaming a million other ways up, *any* other way up except through Jesus is a Babel—the birthplace of the flesh where we start doing a bunch of activities that the Spirit isn't resting on. Pioneers, what you birth in the flesh can only be sustained by the flesh.

It's very hard for Westerners, especially, to understand the concept of kingdom and lordship. We're very keen on leaning on our own understanding, but there are no self-made men in the kingdom. A lot of earthly success is achieved that way but not one single person will enter heaven that way. Pentecost came down to crush the confusion that Babel had raised up. Now we have the mind of Christ to know that anything we resurrect in our lives and ministries that God didn't initiate is a crumbling tower.

The danger of maturity is that we can easily start to settle into self-sufficiency or Babel building. You can never find the will of God by going outside of His will to get it. The beauty of the gospel is it causes me to get over myself and all the Babels I build to try to achieve things outside of His will. Self-sufficiency will always cause us to miss out on the beauty of depending on Jesus. We couldn't possibly lead our lives better than He does.

We're not leading people to our ministries. We're leading them to Jesus. And you have gifts that are quite irrevocable that are for *service* in His kingdom. Ministry is Holy Spirit-empowered service voluntarily flowing in and out of a believer for the strengthening of the whole body of Christ. You may be coming out of a heavy season of warfare, and you're standing in front of a mountain that the Lord is asking you to climb: *Come up here and see what I want to do.* You can't go back, and you can't stay where you've been. The way forward is up, and you're not climbing the mountain alone.

I climbed a mountain with some friends a few years ago. It was an eight-mile round trip from the summit back down to base camp. Elevation was 7,244 feet, and toward the summit, there was a 1,100-foot gain. It probably isn't too hard for an experienced climber, but for an anemic, out-of-shape human, with short legs and lungs with low oxygen capacity, it was a challenge. Ha-ha! The closer I got to the top the heavier everything began to feel. An apple might as well have been an elephant. Everything was so heavy closer to the top. A friend who was a more seasoned climber grabbed my bag, and I was able to make it the rest of the way up. And the view from the top was worth the pain.

I can't think of a better picture of how spiritual gifts function in the body of Christ. Your gifts strengthen me, and my gifts strengthen you. It's a beautiful exchange of mutual submission and shared responsibility. It's leaning over to our brothers and sisters and saying, "Let me help you carry that up the mountain. I want to see you go the distance. I have a tool that can help make this easier for you."

For gifts to be healthy in a church, there cannot be competition and silos and self-protection. There can't be jealousy and contentions and strife and self-promotion. We're called to prefer others above ourselves. Selfish ambition has to die, or it will kill any momentum God wants to establish in your team. We are called to advance the kingdom *together*. That means promoting, supporting, encouraging, and protecting one another. Not just in *your* church. But *the church*.

Culture says, "How can my gifts benefit me." Team Jesus says, "How can my gifts benefit the whole family." We may bring some of those old mindsets with us when we step into this new life in Christ, but they can't stay with us. We have to put them to death. Putting yourself at the top of a pyramid sounds fun until you realize a pyramid is a tomb that holds dead things. Our gifts should be rooted in love for Christ and love for one another. When it becomes about anything other than love, stuff comes unhinged. God is raising up apostolic birthing centers for fully equipped, deeply rooted, Spirit-empowered pioneers, and this is a season of holy alignment.

CULTURE SAYS, "HOW CAN MY GIFTS BENEFIT ME." TEAM JESUS SAYS, "HOW CAN MY GIFTS BENEFIT THE WHOLE FAMILY."

He must increase. Our agendas and flesh must decrease. Our corporate consumeristic mindsets have to go. The church is not an industry. That's a sermon we can all preach, but living it out proves to be more challenging. We can't carry our self-promotion and notoriety up this mountain. We need clean hands and pure hearts. Kingdoms are clashing. You were born into war. It's time to throw off Saul's armor, mature in our Christlikeness, steward the anointing resting on our lives, store the oil of intimacy in the secret place, get our motives pure, and increase in our spiritual authority. God is raising up a purified, positioned priesthood to serve Him:

> Just as our bodies have many parts and each part has a special function, so it is with Christ's body. We are

many parts of one body, and we all belong to each other. In his grace, God has given us different gifts for doing certain things well. So if God has given you the ability to prophesy, speak out with as much faith as God has given you. If your gift is serving others, serve them well. If you are a teacher, teach well. If your gift is to encourage others, be encouraging. If it is giving, give generously. If God has given you leadership ability, take the responsibility seriously. And if you have a gift for showing kindness to others, do it gladly. Don't just pretend to love others. Really love them. Hate what is wrong. Hold tightly to what is good. Love each other with genuine affection, and take delight in honoring each other. Never be lazy, but work hard and serve the Lord enthusiastically.
—Romans 12:4-11 (NLT)

We took our youngest son to play laser tag for his birthday. A computer randomly selected the teams. My husband Eric and oldest son, Josiah, were on team green. David and Judah (our middle and youngest sons) and I were on team red. Usually, Eric and Josiah would separate to make things fair because they're the biggest. But this time, it was the underdogs versus the champions. Ha-ha! As we were getting to the end of our time, I noticed I had negative points. Apparently, I hadn't been shooting the gun right the whole time. Things were not looking hopeful. I made up some lost ground toward the end but still not enough to bring us a win. The event ended, and the announcer came over the speaker, "Red wins! Team red wins!"

I looked at the scoreboard confused how that could be possible because two people from my team had negative individual points, and both Eric and Josiah had thousands of points. Overall though, we had more points. The referee said something that struck me in my spirit: "They were great individually, but you guys were the stronger team because you conquered more territory. Therefore, you won." How true is that when it comes to spiritual gifts and ministry? We can go fast alone. We can use our gifts and make a big fat name for ourselves. But we can conquer more territory when we stick together and work as a team. There is no us versus them. No us versus the church down the street. It's only ever us *and* them.

First Corinthians 12:4-7 (NLT) explains it this way:

There are different kinds of spiritual gifts, but the same Spirit is the source of them all. There are different kinds of service, but we serve the same Lord. God works in different ways, but it is the same God who does the work in all of us. A spiritual gift is given to each of us so we can help each other. Different spiritual gifts are given to every believer so that we can help each other. How can I be Christlike with my gifts in a way that builds you up? The Dead Sea is dead because it always pulls in but never pours out. Believers were not made to always pull in ministry but never pour it back out: "Every believer has received grace gifts, so use them to serve one another as faithful stewards of the many-colored tapestry of God's grace" (1 Peter 4:10, TPT).

4 TRUTHS ABOUT GIFTS:

1) God gives them.
2) We don't pick them.
3) Man can't toss them in the woodchipper.
4) We can use them for the wrong kingdom, though.

God releases these gifts to the body, so we can be healthy, mature, and full of love and Christlike fruit. Gifts protect the church from deception and call the church higher where there's immaturity. It's ministry to the body of Christ and ministry to Christ as the Head of that body. First Corinthians 12:24-25 (TPT) says this: "God has mingled the body parts together, giving greater honor to the "lesser" members who lacked it." He has done this intentionally so that every member would look after the others with mutual concern, and so that there will be no division in the body. There are various spiritual gifts listed throughout the Bible and given to the church. A very important part of being in this priesthood is knowing the part you play and the position you're called to—not because it makes you more important but because we can't grow what we don't even know we have. The next few pages are a quick overview of some of the gifts operating in the church. As God is leading you to pioneer a new path, He also wants to take you on a journey of knowing His heart for you on a deeper level. Any journey of self-discovery should only lead you into deeper intimacy with the Father.

These are *examples* and not an exhaustive list as many gifts aren't listed in scripture. My husband has cooked meals that were so good it felt like Jesus was hugging my soul. I'm pretty sure the heavens opened, and I saw angels. That gift isn't listed in Scripture, but did God give him a special grace to minister to people through food that He did not give me? YEP! You probably have some of those kinds of gifts too—and they matter!

Gifts are generally broken up into three different categories:
1) Serving Gifts = Works That Serve the Bride
2) Speaking Gifts = Words That Serve the Bride
3) Supernatural Gifts = Signs That Serve the Bride

Regardless of the type of gift, they all *serve*. Some serving gift examples in Scripture would be faith, giving, help, administration, discernment, hospitality, mercy, and craftsmanship. If this rings true for you, what a gift you are to the body! You don't just have a gift. YOU ARE A GIFT. You are the hands and feet of Jesus going, building, helping, and ministering His love through your sacrificial deeds. It's worship to Jesus, and it's beautiful care for His beloved.

REGARDLESS OF THE TYPE OF GIFT, THEY ALL SERVE.

The first biblical account of someone being filled with the Spirit of God happened to be an artist and craftsman supernaturally infused with a power that wasn't his own, equipping Him to be a master at every kind of craftsmanship:

> "Look, I have specifically chosen Bezalel son of Uri, grandson of Hur, of the tribe of Judah. I have filled him with the Spirit of God, giving him great wisdom, ability, and expertise in all kinds of crafts."
> —Exodus 31:2-3 (NLT)

I see that same kind of grace on our youngest son, Judah. Everything He tinkers with turns to gold. My vacuum broke—the best vacuum I've ever owned. It wouldn't even start. I sucked up some sand that had spilled, and the tiny particles got sucked into places they shouldn't have. *Whoopsies!* I cleaned it out really well, but it still wouldn't start. I went to the store to get groceries, and while I was gone, Judah got it on his heart to try to fix it for me by himself. This momma came home to a perfectly working vacuum cleaner because my little boy understood his gifts are for *serving*.

When we need to laugh, my oldest son has a gift of exhortation, and just being around him leaves us feeling loved and encouraged. My middle son, David, has gifts of leadership, and when things need to be done, he's just on top of it. Leading by example. Gifts aren't just for your church. Gifts are for *family*. Jesus is so kind to surround us with people who are strong where we are weak. We just get a whole lot more done for the kingdom that way.

Some speaking gift examples from Scripture would be the apostles, prophets, teachers, pastors, evangelists, encouragement, leadership, wisdom, knowledge, and worship. A lot of the gifts I operate in fall into this category. If that's you, too, you are the person who is never short on edifying words for the body. It's a supernatural grace that serves the bride by expressing the Father's heart through words that build up and words that sometimes, have to tear things down. When I was a little girl, a teacher told my parents that I could write a whole novel about the eye of a needle. That teacher had a teaching gift, and because she used her gift well, it awakened the gift inside of me. That is the power of gifts. When we use them well, it gives others permission to do the same.

If used for the wrong kingdom, these gifts can also cause damage. I think the Lord's refining process feels a little more extreme here because of the damage we can cause if we're not submitted to His lordship. I've walked through seasons where I felt like I've lived in His furnace and should probably just start having my mail sent there. The fire isn't punishment. It's purifying your message. We see a fisherman named Peter (whose words often got him into trouble) filled with the Spirit at Pentecost speak a message to the crowd that was so anointed three thousand people gave their lives to Christ, and the church was born.

Just because speaking is not your gift doesn't mean you don't have to open your mouth and declare some things. Your best sermon is your testimony with Jesus. You might not have the gift of evangelism, but Jesus commissioned you to go into all the earth and preach the good news of the gospel. So it's really important that we stay aligned with the Word of God and not use the whole "It's not my gift" rationale as an excuse to be disobedient.

There are also supernatural gifts. A few examples in Scripture would be miracles, healing, prophecy, words of knowledge, tongues/interpretation, dreams/interpretation, and visions. Again, Scripture offers examples; this is not an exhaustive list. I've heard it said before that supernatural gifts are His super resting on our natural. On our own, there is nothing super about it. But *WITH* Him, these gifts reveal His power and defy natural laws which have governed the universe since its creation. Animals speaking, seas splitting, wounded bodies healing, dead men living, demons fleeing, angels appearing all point to a God who defies human logic. He is beyond time and space, and the miracles, signs, and wonders we see still active on the earth evoke the fear of the Lord and testify that God is sovereign Creator over ALL His creation.

Sign gifts don't just do something; they point to Someone and reveal the true nature of the kingdom we belong to. These gifts build our faith, soften hearts to receive Jesus, and call us into alignment with what heaven values. Broken bodies are healed because heaven doesn't know death or sickness. Every miracle is a small taste of what's coming forever. We don't seek signs; we seek God. All of it points back to Him, and there is more than we know: "Jesus also did many other things. If they were all written down, I suppose the whole world could not contain the books that would be written" (John 21:25, NLT), and John 20:30-31 (NLT) says:

> The disciples saw Jesus do many other miraculous signs in addition to the ones recorded in this book. But these are written so that you may continue to believe that Jesus is the Messiah, the Son of God, and that by believing in him you will have life by the power of his name

We are body, soul, and spirit creations. Jesus didn't just die to save us from hell. He died to get heaven in us so we could experience healing and wholeness in our body, soul, AND spirit. One time, my husband and I were doing marriage counseling with a couple in our church. As I was praying for them, my husband started crying because God miraculously healed his ears. They had caused him pain and trouble since he was a young boy, and that day, they just miraculously popped open. We had prayed a lot for that, but in that particular moment, it was the furthest thing from my mind. How and when God moves is not up to us to understand. But we've seen Him move so many times it would take a lot more faith to NOT believe in miracles.

I think it's significant that a doctor named Luke wrote 27.5 percent of the New Testament. Close friends with Paul, Luke probably helped him tremendously in his moments of suffering, as Paul called him a "beloved physician." Luke recorded many verified accounts of healings and miracles through Jesus and other believers. proving that science and faith actually *both* belong to God and aren't in conflict at all.

He conquered death, hell, and the grave. He cursed the curse that was cursing us forever. Healings can and do happen, according to Isaiah 53:5 (NLT), "But he was pierced for our rebellion, crushed for our sins. He was beaten so we could be whole. He was whipped so we could be healed." Miracles can and do happen.

God is still speaking to His prophets. God is still giving dreams because God is the same yesterday, today, and forever. Jesus gives gifts. Salvation. The Holy Spirit. (Who also gives gifts.) And Jesus Himself is a gift! He also gives us the gifts of the prophets, evangelists, apostles, teachers, and pastors to equip the saints for the work of the ministry.

What does any of this have to do with being kingdom pioneers? Absolutely everything because pioneers are tasked with leading the church back to God's original design for how we use our gifts. Too many have used them as a way to advance themselves. We've treated the church like our personal talent agency, and we need to return to God's heart for gifts and how they operate in the life of a believer. Pioneers show us how to use our gifts outside the walls of the church, in culture, and around tables.

The Five-Fold Ministry gifts (not a term you'll find in Scripture but a phrase we use to describe the apostles, prophets, evangelists, teachers, and shepherds) aren't called to *DO* the work of the ministry. They're called to *equip* the saints to do the work of the ministry and to establish governmental order that keeps our houses healthy and fruitful.

Equippers have to transition from demonstrating the power of God to equipping others to operate in it. This is a great shift happening in the body of Christ right now. We're not all called to the office of equipper, but we're all called to equip somebody. Governmental mantles are not operating in their true function if they are not equipping and reproducing. I may have the office of an equipper in the body of Christ, but equipping my sons to be everything Jesus has called them to be and calling them up to their royal destiny is one of the most noble callings on my life. Hidden ministry is just as holy as the public, and the legacy and fruit is longer lasting. Investing time into your family isn't a distraction from ministry. It *is* the most important ministry you will ever be a part of.

I would be devastated to have spent all these many years filling our home with His presence, sharing biblical insights and prophetic revelation, and hearing the voice of God for my family but realizing we carried the load as parents and never equipped our children to do what we do. Don't let your legacy be buried in the ground with you. Pass it to your children.

Teach them to pass it on to their own children. If you don't have children, find some spiritual children and pass it on to them.

When our sons have prophetic dreams or insight, we do not dismiss it as if they have some twisted junior version of the Holy Spirit. We don't mock them or downplay what they're hearing or sharing because they have the full measure of the same Holy Spirit we have. We teach them to lean into the voice of God and to get the solutions of heaven for themselves. I fear the Lord and respect who He is in my children. When something is off with what they're hearing, we pastor them into biblical alignment.

Some of us have traded willingness to pastor a mess for the appearance of a squeaky clean house, and the cost is true discipleship. Reformation looks like family, and nothing can be as messy and beautiful as family. True discipleship causes us to get real about our condition. You can heal, or you can hide but, you can't do both at the same time.

And this is how we should be leading our churches in this hour. As mothers and fathers launching equipped sons and daughters into every sphere of culture. If Sister Sally or Brother Bill is the only one with a prophetic word every week, the principle of equipping the saints for the priesthood may be missing from your house. God's heart is that mothers and fathers would raise up sons and daughters.

I read a statistic somewhere that said 94 percent of churches have a shepherd (gathering, keeping, discipling) model. Only about 6 percent of churches have an apostolic (sending, equipping, pioneering) model. If that's accurate, 94 percent are dying from the moment they are born because they're never reproducing outside of the walls of their own church. There are so many kingdom voices writing, creating, and producing for the crowd when our gifts were made for the throne.

Last summer we were driving by a Chick-fil-A, and their drive-thru was super top-notch. They had a canopy with fans to keep employees cool in the heat and customers dry when they were ordering their food. At first glance it looked overboard, but then I realized the people who thought of that were operating in extraordinary gifts of hospitality and shepherding their employees by caring for their health and safety.

They were influencing culture outside the walls of where we think spiritual gifts should stay. Believers should be the influencers of culture. We have the creative genius of Jesus living inside of us. So why do we try to keep Him boxed into a tiny form when maybe God is wanting to move the gifts out into the most ordinary parts of our lives? What if the church occupied every sphere of influence? Wouldn't that be something?

GOD ISN'T ONLY MOVING IN YOUR HOUSE. HE IS MOVING YOU OUT OF YOUR HOUSE.

It's time to unleash the wild pioneers. To merge the John the Baptists and John the Beloveds. To see people released into every unique kingdom purpose they were created for. We need both expressions equally functioning to have a healthy house. Different. Equally important. God isn't only moving in your house. He is moving you *OUT* of your house. Paul and

Barnabas were *sent* out from the house they were gathered in by the Holy Spirit.

Apostles are *sent* ones. If all roads lead in but never out, the sheep are happy and safe, but a lot of territory is lost in the exchange. Apostolic houses launch flaming arrows of reformation into every sphere and realm of influence. There has to be a coming together of the apostolic and the pastoral. God wants to give us a new mind about what His church should be, what it was always *meant* to be. Pastors gather. Apostles send out. We need both.

It's not that God isn't moving. Maybe God is moving you OUT—out of the walls and out of the programs. The more we step out of the idolization of forms and into family the more we'll shift into the apostolic heart of the Father. Apostolic houses are greenhouses. Incubators of kingdom purpose. God is building an apostolic family that is big enough and safe enough for every single believer to step into the fullness of what heaven has spoken over their life. Nothing will frustrate an apostolic heart like an old wineskin and a box.

A huge part of this reformation is allowing God to realign our ecclesiology back to His heart. As helpful as they can be, we can make personality tests and spiritual gifts tests a form of idolatry. This isn't condemnation; it's good to be self-aware. It's a gentle reminder that we do not worship gifts, platforms, personalities, or people. We worship the Giver, and we follow the Giver. Even Paul said, "Follow me as I follow Christ" (1 Corinthians 11:1, author paraphrase). Is the person you're following leading you closer to Christ? Are the people following you coming closer to Jesus or closer to your vision?

Cessationists believe that the sign gifts of the Spirit (miracles, healings, speaking in tongues, private prophetic revelation, casting out demons, etc.) have stopped and are no longer relevant for the church. Continuationists believe that the sign gifts of the Spirit continue and will not stop this side of eternity and that the Spirit *still* works through gifts such as prophecy, knowledge, tongues, and healings in various ways. Continuationists are also referred to as being charismatic or Pentecostal. Whether you know it or not, God has given you a unique ministry ability modeled after Jesus and distributed to the whole church through the power of the Holy Spirit so that you can effectively serve others with that gift.

Why does any of that information matter? Because it's important that you know the things you read about in the book of Acts never came with an expiration date for the church. Paul tells the church in Ephesus that the gifts will continue until we reach perfect unity and Christlikeness. Jesus never would have left us with a commission that requires spiritual gifts unless He meant for us to use them. When do spiritual gifts end? Not until we ALL look like Jesus. So, not on *this* side of eternity.

Every believer is in a process called sanctification. We're looking more like Jesus day by day. We're repenting. Which is more than just an apology; it's getting a completely new mind about something. It's keeping a knife to our flesh. None of us has arrived at perfection. Paul tells us when it comes to spiritual gifts not to be uninformed. God doesn't just give us gifts, but He wants to train our hands for war and teach us to use them in a way that builds others up in unity, faith, and maturity until He comes:

> Now these are the gifts Christ gave to the church: the apostles, the prophets, the evangelists, and the pastors and teachers. Their responsibility is to equip God's people to do his work and build up the church, the body of Christ. This will continue until we all come to such unity in our faith and knowledge of God's Son that we will be mature in the Lord, measuring up to the full and complete standard of Christ.
> —Ephesians 4:11-13 (NLT)

TAKE AWAY JESUS, AND THE GIFT IS STILL ACTIVE, BUT THE ANOINTING HAS LEFT THE BUILDING.

That means we need to STOP using our gifts to compare, compete, and beat our brothers and sisters upside the head. Using tools as weapons is dangerous. Without submitting to His lordship in our lives, the right gift is being anointed under the wrong banner. Take away Jesus, and the gift is still active, but the anointing has left the building. God doesn't take our gifts away. But we can use them for the wrong kingdom. Anytime we take one step outside of Scripture, we're well on our way in that direction. God wants to train you to use your gifts in a way that is an asset and blessing—not a liability and danger. He wants pure ministry flowing through our lives.

Nothing hinders the flow of the Spirit on our gifts like jealousy. Just read James 3:16 (TPT) to see that: "Wherever jealousy and selfishness are uncovered, you will also find many troubles and every kind of meanness." Jealousy is a busy spirit that wears a lot of faces. When our gifts are yielded to the Holy Spirit, we start to discern healthy things from the right kingdom like God's favor and grace on people. When our gifts are healthy, they pull people into divine alignment. When our gifts are not healthy, they cause deep hurts and division. Gifts without good fruit hurt people. They misrepresent Jesus. We need to invite Jesus to purify our gifts, so they are a sweet aroma to Him and the reflection of His heart to the body they were meant to be.

It's not about my gift, position, title, church, or even my clout. It's about your need. How can I use my gifts in a way that brings you into connection with the Father? If you know your gifts or you take a free spiritual gifts test online after reading this, just know that gifts are not badges of how Christlike you are. The devil had abilities too. It's not what you have. It's how you use it. Are you using your gifts to serve yourself, in partnership with the accuser to attack parts of the body or for the bride He loves? This is the era of returning to His heart. Valuing what He values. It's a total reformation of how we view ministry and gifts.

HEALTHY MINISTRY MINDSETS:
    GET TO > HAVE TO
    EVERYDAY > SUNDAY
    LIFESTYLE > EVENT
    FRUIT > FORM
    TABLES > STAGES
    MOTHERS + FATHERS > TITLES
    SONS + DAUGHTERS > NUMBERS

DISCIPLESHIP > MEMBERSHIP
SENDING > STAYING
PRIVATE MINISTRY > PUBLIC MINISTRY
FAITHFUL > FAMOUS
ROOTED > RELEVANT
PURITY > PERFORMANCE

Anything we do that isn't for Jesus and His bride or any other agenda dies with us when we die. Heaven isn't distributing awards for the platforms we build. That desire is going to turn to ash after we enter glory. So how do we identify healthy churches when performance and consumerism have been the gold standard for so long? We return to Scripture.

HEALTHY HOUSES (ACCORDING TO EPHESIANS 4)

- » Have biblically qualified healthy leaders.
- » Have equipped believers living out the priesthood.
- » There's a collective pursuit of honor, love, and unity.
- » There's a continual pursuit of Christlike maturity.

SIGNS OF A BIBLICALLY HEALTHY MINISTRY:

- » There is a call from God.
- » There are spiritual gifts actively working to serve.
- » There is an anointing on the believer.
- » There is good fruit to sustain it.
- » Leads people to Jesus—not our personalities.
- » Equips people to hear God for themselves.

- » Produces Christlikeness.
- » Is always aligned to Scripture.

4 SIGNS YOU ARE GROWING IN YOUR GIFTS:

1) You receive loving correction without taking it as a personal attack.
2) You're not attaching your identity or value to your assignments in ministry.
3) Christlikeness is the new gold standard.
4) You're being led by the Spirit of God.

Planted seeds grow. Tumbleweeds blow. We are called to be planted in a house. Sometimes, there are rare seasons when God calls us into a wilderness, but that is only meant to be a season. Anything healthy God does will happen in community. God has called us to be planted, fed, and flourishing in a healthy house. (See Psalms 92:12-13 and Hebrews 10:25.) Offense causes believers to disconnect from the church like tumbleweeds blowing from one house to the next, one doctrine to the next. Jesus said every plant not planted by the Father is destined to be uprooted. But as children of God, we are called to be a planted people—planted in the body of Christ and planted in a healthy house.

Tumbleweeds run from correction and conflict, and because they never get to the root of the issue, it follows them from house to house. Offense causes us to leave home instead of leaning into the correction and loving discipline of the Lord that would shape us for the future God has for us. (See Hebrews

12:10.) Being released and sent is biblical. In Acts 13:2-3 Barnabas and Paul were gathered with a group of believers in the middle of fasting and worship when the Holy Spirit called them to go on their first missionary journey. So they prayed some more, laid hands on them, released them, and the rest is history.

Uprooting over offense is not biblical but all too common in the church. Uprooting over preferences is also not biblical. There are so many options that we shop for churches like we shop for new socks. The first snag, and we throw it out and buy another. Consumers are professional church shoppers, but this isn't the life Jesus called us to live. This is also a side effect of creating consumer-driven church models. (1 Corinthians 1:10) Jesus is building ONE thing. He has no plan B. It's just His church, and if you've given Him your heart, you're part of that church and a minister. Wherever God calls you, man sends you, or you leave to by personal choice—be ALL there.

WHEREVER GOD CALLS YOU, MAN SENDS YOU, OR YOU LEAVE TO BY PERSONAL CHOICE—BE ALL THERE.

Commit. Don't be a tumbleweed Christian forever, bouncing from house to house because it doesn't serve you, the kingdom, or anybody. Go when you're sent. Go when it's too toxic to stay. We'll have literally FOREVER AND EVER to catch up one day. I want your church to make it to the end because we're family with different assignments, so the gospel can go further than we could ever take it alone. Leaving without being sent is a scary place to be. It's a cult waiting to happen when we choose isolation. You're not exiled. You're called to family.

What if there were a whole lot we could learn from each other if we stopped treating other churches like competition or using houses of worship like weapons to retaliate, instead of working out our differences in biblical ways? We miss out on so much growth when we cancel people. God cannot use tumbleweeds—only planted seeds. Wherever you are planted, it won't be easy because churches have people, and people are people (and so are you), but it's still worth it. Be fully committed to the house you're planted in. It takes deeply rooted maturity to keep building where you're planted in spite of offense or different opinions and to stay faithful to the season when your heart is somewhere else. How you leave a season matters to God. Read Nehemiah and his relationship with the king. There is a big difference between leaving and being sent.

Honor the pastors of the church you're planted in. It's been said that God treats churches how churches treat their pastors. I think there's truth to that. Serve with your gifts, love with your whole heart, tithe to the house you're planted in, and go deep in connection. Don't be a spectator. It's time to put your hand to the plow. Instead of searching for a perfect church in humility and honor, commit to bringing kingdom solutions to the things that bother you. That's probably why you're passionate about it to begin with. There are seasons to rest and reset, but those seasons have an expiration date. It may be time to switch from consumer to contributor. Instead of complaining about what your church lacks, meet that need, and make the church body whole:

> Then we will no longer be immature like children. We won't be tossed and blown about by every wind of new teaching. We will not be influenced when people try to trick us with lies so clever they sound like the truth. Instead, we will speak the truth in love, growing in every way more and more like Christ, who is the head of his body, the church. He makes the whole body fit together perfectly. As each part does its own special work, it helps the other parts grow, so that the whole body is healthy and growing and full of love. —Ephesians 4:14-16 (NLT)

Sometimes, church hurt causes us to take on the nature of a tumbleweed. Tumbleweeds burst into flames and spread dangerous fires everywhere they blow. They cause accidents and spread viruses to healthy crops. They start as plants with flowering fruit that nourishes, but then they dry up and detach from their roots. They soak up water everywhere they go, but never give any back. God hasn't called any tumbleweed Christians. He wants firmly planted giants: "They will be like great oaks that the Lord has planted for his own glory" (Isaiah 61:3, NLT).

Maybe you deeply loved the church at one time and tried to be planted in a house, but genuine abuses have caused you to harden your heart and put up walls so thick you struggle to even imagine a reality where those walls no longer exist. You stopped trusting institutions. If that's your story, I'm so sorry.

God doesn't require you to stay in a church that is toxic or physically, sexually, or spiritually abusive. He doesn't call you to stay in a house that preaches a different gospel than the Bible. He doesn't call you to stay planted in a church that manipulates, rejects, attacks, accuses, controls, and destroys. He doesn't call you to hide sin to protect leaders behaving badly. You're not the problem. It was wrong, and maybe you just need someone to tell you that. You're not crazy. What happened to you was wrong.

Church should be the safest place in the world for your family, and I pray you find a healthy house to heal in. They are out there, and I hope this book shows you how to find them. I've had to get my fair share of counseling, deliverance, and inner healing from all the church hurt I've both caused and experienced. We all have pasts and stories. You're not alone.

Processing your pain privately with safe people in safe spaces will help you move forward instead of being held hostage by those events. Getting help is not the weak path. It's the biblical path. Institutions and people fail every day. I've failed. You've failed. None of it is okay, and that statement isn't a "Get out of jail free" card for all the wrong done against you. But may it be encouragement to your soul as you rest in the reality that Jesus never fails. His banner over you is love, and you are beloved.

HIS BANNER OVER YOU IS LOVE, AND YOU ARE BELOVED.

Men can try to take away your assignment. They can close doors. They can treat you unfairly. They can gossip, plot, and strategize to shut you down. They can take credit for things you've built from the ground up. They can wound and shoot arrows of accusation against you. But they can't touch your freedom in Christ. They can't take the rewards of your labor. They can't stop you from staying Christlike. They can't take your inheritance. They can't touch your salvation. They can't keep you from the land you're called to occupy. They can't control your fruit. They can't muzzle your voice. In the end, you still win. You're heading to a wedding. What else matters?

The wilderness with Jesus is better than all the stages of striving and platforms of performance. Jesus is so much better my friends. You could lose it all and still have everything. You get to spend your hours and days loving Jesus and being loved by Him. Pouring your oil on Him. Listening to the chain-breaking melodies the Father sings over your heart. Bathing in the truth of every word He's ever spoken. Warring with those prophesies. Knowing His heart. Ministering to Him. Receiving His ministry. Fully known and fully loved. Beautiful things can be birthed accidentally when we simply and purely abide with Jesus. He will never be unfaithful to you. He will never reject you.

You are a royal priesthood. He's the purpose and the prize. Shake off the sleepy dust and awaken again to First Love. A lot was lost from the last season, but you're still standing on everything that matters. Whatever is keeping your eyes off Jesus, is not from Jesus. There's no time to get hung up on things that aren't eternal. Satan and all the demons of hell could have been at this wedding if it weren't for pride. Now he has one goal. To see the church distracted, divided, and ultimately locked out of the wedding too. Don't let your lamp run dry.

It wasn't God who hurt you. We can't violate His Word because misbehaving children used it to hurt us. People fail. His kingdom is unshakable. You are brave to step back into new waters even though your cuts are fresh and everything stings. Even though you're not sure how it will work out or who you can trust. Even though you're still clinging to the pain of what was lost. God sees you trying, and He is not going to let you drown. He will lead you to safe people. He will lead you to the land He's promised.

Sometimes we crave things from the church that we can only find in Jesus—like approval and perfection. Jesus is perfect. The rest of us are a work in progress. Find a healthy church and be faithful to Jesus. We work for Him—not the approval or acceptance of man. The work God has set apart for you to do is holy. Too holy to compare assignments. Too holy to quit because sometimes, sheep bite. We are called to love the sheep (and remember we are one.) There are only imperfect people in this priesthood, and God still chooses to use our gifts.

PLATFORMS ARE LONELIER THAN THEY APPEAR TO BE, BUT IT'S RARE FOR PEOPLE TO TELL THE TRUTH ABOUT THAT BECAUSE WE'RE TOO BUSY MAKING IT SEEM LIKE A MOUNTAINTOP.

Platforms are lonelier than they appear to be, but it's rare for people to tell the truth about that because we're too busy making it seem like a mountaintop. Stages and microphones flood our Instagram accounts, and it's confusing. It seems like that's the prize. But believe me, Jesus is the only prize. Don't be impressed by status. Heaven isn't. There is a difference between public ministry and private ministry. Not every gift is meant to be publicly expressed. It's a wild river, but there are boundary lines the Lord has established. Private ministry builds up ourselves. (See Jude 1:20.) Public ministry builds up others. (See Ephesians 4:12.) There is a time and place for both.

SHOULD I USE MY GIFTS IN GATHERINGS? (1 CORINTHIANS 14)

- » Does it truthfully and lovingly represent God?
- » Will it edify and build up the church?
- » Will it encourage and bring comfort or fear?
- » Is this a word for THIS season?
- » Are my motives pure?
- » Am I accurately Handling scripture? Will it help or hinder?

Jesus already gave us the greatest gifts we'll ever receive, but finding out your spiritual gifts feels a lot like Christmas morning. Smell the breakfast cooking and the hot coffee brewing. The smell of a fresh-cut Christmas tree. The house is quiet. You look under the glowing tree, and there are beautifully packaged gifts from your Father. Your name is on them. Now it's time to open the gifts. What now?

If you've ever taken a free spiritual gifts assessment online, don't overthink it, but try to view yourself as honestly and accurately as possible and not through the lens of what you *wish* you could have. We didn't send Jesus a Christmas list. He gave us what *He* wanted us to have, and He knows the reason why. Gifts are for serving the church, and gifts are for Him, His pleasure and glory, and the advancement of HIS kingdom.

The priestly mantle you walk in protects what God values. It's a call to His presence. We should celebrate every gift. Every sold-out stadium could be full of hungry burning hearts, but as His royal priesthood, our *first* ministry will always be to worship and love Him. Our highest calling is inner court ministry to Jesus. Our marriage and children are next. Everything else comes last. God doesn't just want to be first in your life. He is Lord. He wants to be Lord of ALL. Lord over our marriage. Lord over our finances. Lord over our daily plans. Lord over what we're watching. Lord over what we're speaking. Lord of ALL.

SPIRITUAL GIFTS STEWARDSHIP TIPS:
» Research the biblical makeup of your gift.
» Research biblical people who have your gift.
» Research historical people who had your gift.
» Study the strengths AND weaknesses of your gift.
» How did Jesus model your gift?

FURTHER QUESTIONS (LOOK FOR PATTERNS AND SIMILARITIES):
» Where do you sense the joy of Christ?
» Where have others witnessed your effectiveness?
» What grieves your spirit most?
» What could you talk about for hours?
» What prophesies have been spoken over you?

- » What has the Holy Spirit spoken over you?
- » What abilities has God given you?
- » What do you see that others often overlook?
- » Is there a common reason people seek you out?
- » What's in your hand that could serve someone?
- » How has God refined your character?
- » How has Jesus changed your life and set you free?

WHAT'S NEXT?

- » Learn to use a mop before you use a microphone.
- » Don't love your platform more than your people.
- » Don't expect a harvest where you didn't plant one.
- » Steward the small hidden things well.
- » Rest. Store oil. Protect the Anointing. Don't quit.
- » Crave the altar more than the stage.
- » Remember who our gifts are really for.

When you discover your gift, the journey doesn't end there. You're now responsible for stewarding and growing in that gift for the rest of your life here on this earth. The point of our gifts is to point people to Jesus. He is the only topic.

WHEN YOU DISCOVER YOUR GIFT, THE JOURNEY DOESN'T END THERE. YOU'RE NOW RESPONSIBLE FOR STEWARDING AND GROWING IN THAT GIFT FOR THE REST OF YOUR LIFE HERE ON THIS EARTH.

Gifts are great, but what a feast it is just to be near Him. Kids love Christmas gifts, but it's a parent's delight to be in the room when they are opened. There are wild pleasures to belong to Christ. He rejoices in seeing you discover who He has created you to be. He loves to see you open the gifts, but comparison is the Grinch that stole Christmas. It kills creativity and joy. Run your own race well with your eyes on the prize. Jesus, our great High Priest, said, "It is finished," and ended the sacrificial system. He really, truly meant it. He became the sacrifice. So now it's our HIGHEST delight to simply love Him and be loved by Him, consumed until He comes, and then forever: "Zeal for your house consumes me" (Psalm 69:9, NIV).

> **PIONEER PRAYER:**
> *Jesus, Your bride is lovely and full of expectancy for Your return. Holy Spirit, make me ready and radiant. High Priest of heaven, You split the curtain, so there's no returning to the bondage of the old system. I am a priest in Your priesthood, and I say yes. Yes to holy hard work. Yes to loving what you love. Yes to cleaning the inside of the cup. Yes to the removal of mixture from my house. Yes to reformation. Yes to the harvest fields and yes to the mess. Yes to the purifying and pruning and pain. Use every gift I have for your glory alone. I give each one back as worship to You. Be glorified in Your church and through my life forever and ever. Amen.*

Pioneer Prompt:

After you take a free spiritual gifts assessment online (just Google one) ask the Lord to reveal how your specific gifts can pioneer paths for others to encounter His wild love both inside and outside the walls of the church. Journal His responses. If you're already aware of your gifts, are they only operational on Sunday? How is God wanting to use them outside of the four walls of the church, to your family, and places of influence?

___

___

___

___

___

___

___

___

___

___

___

___

CHAPTER 7

The Pioneer

eing a pioneer sounds so attractive until you realize it means taking the first deep cuts. Laboring for a land you can't see. Pushing through intense pressure. Showing up when you don't feel like you can take another step forward. Caring when nobody else seems to care. Leading others where they don't want to follow to a promised land they'll probably get to enjoy without you. Being the invisible foundation others will build on and get all the glory for. Clearing the path so others coming after you have it easier. Dying to comfort and popularity. Discovering a million ways to make something *not* work. Failing and choosing to try again. Sometimes, losing relationships you've spent years investing in and choosing to love like Jesus anyway, knowing there will always be the risk of people walking away. Experiencing warfare on another level. And experiencing it frequently. *Sign me up, right?!*

> **WE ARE CALLED TO EQUIP AND RELEASE PEOPLE INTO THEIR DESTINIES. NOT DOING THAT IS FORSAKING THE ESSENCE OF OUR CALLING AS PIONEERS.**

The apostles and prophets are the foundation of a house, not the roof. They are the foundation, not the top of a hierarchy. If you crave being the top, that could create some tension between you and the Lord if He's called you to be the foundation of something. Forcing people to stay under your lids may have the appearance of self-preservation, but it's actually one of the most self-sabotaging moves a pioneer can make. We are called to equip and release people into their destinies. Not doing *that* is forsaking the essence of our calling as pioneers.

The point of a foundation is for everything else to be built on top of it. For everything around you to grow bigger, better, fuller, and taller. To last longer. When we draw our final breath, the goal should be for whatever we built on this earth to thrive without us. If what you're building can't thrive without you, you're missing the point. If we do it right, a foundation becomes invisible while everyone is increasing and being built up around them. But the Lord sees and rewards everything that was truly built for His glory. Everything else turns to dust anyway.

Good fathers and mothers *WANT* their children to surpass them. At least Paul believed so:

> It is my honor and constant passion to be a pioneer who preaches where no one has ever even heard of the Anointed One, instead of building upon someone else's foundation. —Romans 15:20 (TPT)

If you're operating in a governmental role in the church, you are not called to *just* be the voice of God for the church. You are called to equip the church to hear the voice of God for themselves. Nothing gives more dignity to people than teaching them that they were born to know their Shepherd's voice. Things get twisted when one person in a house becomes the only voice. For example, I have a gift of interpreting dreams. People will often bring me their dreams for insight, and I love getting to share God's heart with people. But if the goal of my life is to be the *only* dream interpreter, I've just robbed hundreds of people of an encounter with Jesus.

The Father, Son, and Spirit are entirely relational. When we run to Google or a book or a person to give meaning to something before we seek the Lord about it, we've robbed God of the very thing He wanted most: connection with the people He loves. There are great resources when He tells you to lean into them, but if we're replacing His voice with man's, we've stopped beholding Jesus. We become what we behold. Now, that thing we're beholding has a hold of us. It has our worship because we're worshipers by design. If our worship isn't going to God, it will always go to something or someone else.

Joseph and Daniel didn't have Google or a dream interpretation book. They had intimacy with a Father who revealed secrets to sons. This is what we are ultimately chasing after as pioneers, and it's a kingdom value HIGH above knowledge and understanding. I think God would rather we live in mystery and connection over a constant awareness of every move He makes but disconnected from the Source. God is okay with the process and letting us wait things out with Him if it leads to time with you. A fresh word can't always be decoded in a book. What means something one time may not mean the same thing the next time. This is why pioneers need to be continually led by the Spirit and not stuck in a formula. I use dreams as an example, but this truth applies to whatever God has called you to pioneer. We can't stay at the top of the ladder. We should continually be investing in people who will surpass us.

WE CAN'T STAY AT THE TOP OF THE LADDER. WE SHOULD CONTINUALLY BE INVESTING IN PEOPLE WHO WILL SURPASS US.

If a person gets jealous and manifests a spirit of control because you run to the counsel of Jesus instead of *them,* that is a big red flag that something is not healthy in that church. Pioneers are not territorial and controlling. They aren't glorified platform protectors. They live sacrificially, thinking of the people who will come behind them above their own comfort and position. Pioneering done well and pure is free of self-promotion. We are joined together, and we rise together. Ministry isn't about who we serve under or being the person on top others serve under. It's about who we're building on.

There is a plurality of fathers and mothers who have invested in my calling. They are not my capstone, and I am not their carbon copy. I take the treasure of what those pioneers invested in my life, and I honor it best by not living as a watered-down version of who they were but by adding it to who the Father has called *me* to be and what He's called me to personally pioneer. This is how the story goes from glory to glory with ever-increasing glory, passing from one generation to the next. This is how His kingdom has no end. This is how Jesus gets His full reward and how we see the increase of His government on the earth. This is how heaven invades earth. This is how kingdom mindsets replace church ones. It's not about building ivory towers; it's a people willing to be at the bottom of one.

It's not about personal recognition; it's about recognizing the gifts in others and properly equipping them and loving them well so they are strengthened to go the distance. Sons and daughters who last and shine brighter in an hour that's only growing darker. It's not about guarding our ministry silos. It's about smashing them to pieces and letting ministry flow outward. For too long, the focus of the church has been inward. Recruiting gifts for our houses instead of equipping people to use their gifts outside of the house where 98 percent of the church spends 98 percent of their time.

Instead, we've mastered the art of equipping 98 percent of believers to use 100 percent of their gifts 2 percent of the time. I flunked math my senior year because I was bored and skipped class too much and had to take summer school to graduate. Now I homeschool my sons and teach them math which I'm currently doing as I write this book. *God help us all.* But even *I* can tell you that equation doesn't add up.

The kingdom isn't meant to stay confined to our institutions. It's meant to spill out and transform culture. Where pioneers pave pathways back to the heart of the Father. Where kings equip believers to overtake the marketplace with kingdom values. Where Levites decline the invitation to prostitute their gifts on platforms of performance. Where evangelists stop propping their egos on packed stadiums and seek the one who needs a drink of living water. Where the teachers leave the classroom and start letting their laid-down lives be the lesson in the presence of sons and daughters. Where the apostles stop trying to find new inventive ways to *keep* consumers entertained and start releasing contributors like flaming arrows of reformation shot into the darkness. Where the pastors break bread with the broken and the hungry are fed solid food around tables where God isn't taking attendance, but nothing is hidden, and nobody is overlooked. Where the church values *personal revival* above personal advancement.

I realized later in life that God was calling me to be a pioneer of His heart. I think a better way to put it would be I was *already* moving in the prophetic and pioneering for years and wondering why I was always so bloody and bruised and going a direction few others seemed called to and discerning things on God's heart that nobody else seemed bothered by. It always felt like I was a step ahead, waiting for everyone to catch up. Like I had a map in my hands of where God was wanting to direct our steps, but I had zero influence or ability to convince others to go there with me.

Why was I always experiencing such intense resistance around my calling? Why was I so unsettled in my spirit with the idea of going through the motions? Why did Christians look at us like we had three eyeballs because of the consecrated way Jesus had called us to raise our family? Why did the risk of the unknown always feel more appealing than being boxed inside religious programs and the traditions of men? I know the answer now. It would have been helpful to know twenty years ago. *Pioneers go first. Our commissioning service happens in the wilderness.*

PIONEERS GO FIRST. OUR COMMISSIONING SERVICE HAPPENS IN THE WILDERNESS.

If any of that feels relatable to your own journey, you may be a pioneer too. I grew up in the woods. I loved nature, and when we weren't working on the farm, I would spend all day exploring our land by myself. I remember skipping down our wooded hills one rainy day and passing a fox den with a momma fox and her pups trying to stay dry from the storm. Looking back, they probably thought Uber Eats had delivered their supper. Ha-ha! I'm so thankful for parents who let me be wild and didn't try to fit me in a mold of what they thought I should be.

Fishing and swimming in the river were our rewards for hard work. Camping was our vacation. I was creative and adventurous and always willing to go first and take risks and try new things. I saw potential where others saw impossibility. I was obnoxiously optimistic. My mom always made my hair pretty and dressed me up, but in almost every childhood picture I own that *wasn't* taken professionally, I was wild, dirty, cut, bruised, blistered, and living my absolute best childhood.

What I didn't realize is that wild childhood was preparing me for a lifetime of *kingdom* pioneering. I clean up well enough for pictures now, but if you could see my soul, it's still pretty wild, dirty, cut, bruised, and blistered, and I'm still having the time of my life following Jesus and leading others into deeper connection with His heart.

WHAT *IS* A KINGDOM PIONEER?

- » They deeply love what God values and want to lead others back to that.
- » They're wild and adventurous.
- » They carry a map others don't see.
- » They break religious boxes to follow that map.
- » They're creative, innovative, and optimistic.
- » They aren't afraid of being uncomfortable.
- » They are fully yielded to the flowing river of God.
- » They see potential where others see a dead end.
- » They go first, take risks, and are covered in scars.
- » Their ears are pressed against the Father's heart, and their only desire is to tell the world what it sounds like.

Now that we've clarified what a kingdom pioneer is, let's also clarify what it's very much NOT.

A KINGDOM PIONEER IS NOT:
- » It's NOT rebellion rooted in church hurt.
- » It's NOT interested in building a name for itself.
- » It's NOT proud and unteachable.
- » It's NOT disconnected from healthy community.
- » It's NOT holding a grudge against institutions.
- » It's NOT accusatory and divisive.
- » It's NOT operating outside of Scripture.
- » It's NOT seeking its own honor.
- » It's NOT idolizing platforms.
- » It's NOT operating with a critical spirit.

Kingdom pioneers love the church deeply and long to see her return to the Father's heart where she's gotten off course. They are not cozy and infatuated with the systems and comforts lulling the bride to sleep. They long to see her return to her wild side before she traded flow charts for flowing rivers. To see the church trade consumer mindsets for kingdom ones. The warfare you face for pioneering is less about you and more about the purity of the wild ones coming up *behind* you. They are the King Josiahs, toppling the idols we've made of ministry, the industry we've made of worship, and the production we've made of the church.

PIONEERING ISN'T A HOBBY WE PICK UP LIKE GOLF. OH, I THINK I WANNA TRY PIONEERING TODAY. IT'S NOT EVEN A SPIRITUAL GIFT. IT'S SIMPLY AN INVITATION TO FOLLOW JESUS INTO THE WILD.

Pioneering isn't a hobby we pick up like golf. *Oh, I think I wanna try pioneering today.* It's not even a spiritual gift. It's simply an invitation to follow Jesus into the wild. It's a returning to God's heart for the church. It's the new wine bursting out of old wineskins. It's an invitation to unusual warfare, pain, invisibility, sacrifice, and the death of your flesh. It's one thing to experience those things by yourself, but when your children start experiencing the pain of pioneering? That's another test entirely. You might find yourself wondering, *God do they know what my children experienced and had to sacrifice for this to happen? Where is the honor?* Our kids are born into war, and all we can do is trust God to train their hands for battle.

Pioneers are the bottom of a great cathedral. Not the cornerstone. Not the capstone. But part of the foundation. Everyone admires the stained glass and the painted ceilings, but without a strong foundation, that building would collapse on everyone inside of it. There would be nothing to build on. Pioneers are protectors of what the Lord is building and protectors of what the Lord values. If you're a pioneer, the rewards are in heaven with the Father. It's in the fruit of seeing what was built outlast you. It's in the health of those who come up after you.

Where was the honor for John the Baptist when he was beheaded? Or when Jesus's sweat turned to blood for our emotions to be healed? Where was the honor when He was disfigured, so we could be His image bearers? When His head was pierced with a crown of thorns, so we could have His mind and be a royal priesthood who lays our crowns at His feet? Where was the honor when they whipped His back so brutally, bone was exposed, and flesh was ripped for our healing? Or when the nails pierced His feet so we could walk in His peace? Where was the honor when His hands were pierced so we could carry reconciliation to the nations? Or when they pierced His side, so we could be born again of blood and water? Where was the honor when He was pulling Himself up for oxygen, so we could be filled with the breath of His Spirit? He didn't do it for honor. He did it for love.

It's not just a memory. It's a love story. Understanding His delight in you will flip your whole life upside down. Nothing about Jesus should be treated as common or familiar. He deserved *all* the honor but chose a cross, and while we're waiting for the esteem of men, He's waiting for us to pick up ours. Not to complete what He already finished. We never want to give power to something Jesus disempowered on the cross. But He is calling us to carry our own cross and that looks different for each of us. Suffering and joy. Glorification and lowliness. They are a drink from the same cup. Jesus asks that we stop bargaining and drink the cup and carry the cross like Jesus did: "I never have a need to seek my own glory, for the Father will do that for me, and he will judge those who do not" (John 8:50, TPT).

Or like our forebears did:

> Therefore, since we are surrounded by such a great cloud of witnesses, let us throw off everything that hinders and the sin that so easily entangles. And let us run with perseverance the race marked out for us, fixing our eyes on Jesus, the pioneer and perfecter of faith. For the joy set before him he endured the cross, scorning its shame, and sat down at the right hand of

the throne of God. Consider him who endured such opposition from sinners, so that you will not grow weary and lose heart. –Hebrews 12:1-3 (NIV)

If you're seeking your own glory and honor, pioneering is not your gig. This isn't the model of the world system. You know you're dealing with mixture if the top of the ladder is the goal of your life. That wasn't the model Jesus gave us when He said we'd do even *greater* things than He did. His model was dying so others could rise with Him:

> In putting everything under them, God left nothing that is not subject to them. Yet at present we do not see everything subject to them. But we do see Jesus, who was made lower than the angels for a little while, now crowned with glory and honor because he suffered death, so that by the grace of God he might taste death for everyone. In bringing many sons and daughters to glory, it was fitting that God, for whom and through whom everything exists, should make the pioneer of their salvation perfect through what he suffered. Both the one who makes people holy and those who are made holy are of the same family. So Jesus is not ashamed to call them brothers and sisters. —Hebrews 2:8-11 (NIV)

The burning desire of every pioneer is to build something that will outlast them, so Jesus can get the full reward of His suffering. They don't care if they get the credit for it. They just want to see the work finished and Jesus get His full reward. They also don't care about instant results. They are obedient to the voice of the Lord for the long haul. They are loyal to the

King alone and moved by every desire of His heart. If you have ever had to pioneer in a direction nobody has gone before, you're in good company:

> Faith opened Noah's heart to receive revelation and warnings from God about what was coming, even things that had never been seen. But he stepped out in reverent obedience to God and built an ark that would save him and his family. By his faith the world was condemned, but Noah received God's gift of righteousness that comes by believing. Faith motivated Abraham to obey God's call and leave the familiar to discover the territory he was destined to inherit from God. So he left with only a promise and without even knowing ahead of time where he was going, Abraham stepped out in faith. He lived by faith as an immigrant in his promised land as though it belonged to someone else. He journeyed through the land living in tents with Isaac and Jacob who were persuaded that they were also co-heirs of the same promise. His eyes of faith were set on the city with unshakable foundations, whose architect and builder is God himself. Sarah's faith embraced God's miracle power to conceive even though she was barren and was past the age of childbearing, for the authority of her faith rested in the One who made the promise, and she tapped into his faithfulness. In fact, so many children were subsequently fathered by this aged man of faith—one who was as good as dead, that he now has offspring as innumerable as the sand on the seashore and as the stars in the sky! These heroes all died still clinging to their faith, not even receiving all that had been promised them. But

> they saw beyond the horizon the fulfillment of their promises and gladly embraced it from afar. They all lived their lives on earth as those who belonged to another realm. For clearly, those who live this way are longing for the appearing of a heavenly city. And if their hearts were still remembering what they left behind, they would have found an opportunity to go back. But they couldn't turn back for their hearts were fixed on what was far greater, that is, the heavenly realm! So because of this God is not ashamed in any way to be called their God, for he has prepared a heavenly city for them. —Hebrews 11:7-16 (TPT)

It requires a reformational mindset to not look back. To keep your eyes focused beyond the horizon. To set sail clinging to a promise you can't see. To die, still not seeing the completion of it. To live an entire lifetime as citizens of another realm. Pioneers holding onto faith, God is not ashamed in *ANY* way to be called your God. Whether your own eyes see it or the generations after you, it will be done according to His will. Every promise will be kept. Every word will be finished to completion.

PIONEERS HOLDING ONTO FAITH, GOD IS NOT ASHAMED IN ANY WAY TO BE CALLED YOUR GOD.

Pioneers are able to multiply themselves in others so well that the greatest joy of their life is to see others reach the land, even if they don't ever see it with their own eyes. They don't live a day making others around them feel small. They value the greatness of who God is in people and know how to pass the baton well. Too many greats have died, and they are still clinging to it. What you don't pass on dies with you. For those who long to be on top, you're going to find yourself frustrated because God is only interested in building a holy foundation from your laid down life—not a pyramid to your greatness. It's no longer about what you build with your own hands but who you're building on and who is building on you. He is sending a plurality of people to influence your life and a plurality of people for you to influence. They will be the foundation you build on—not your capstone or cornerstone, and you will lay a foundation others build on. This is how the lid comes off.

To honor pioneering leaders you build on isn't to pretend you'll never fill their shoes; it's not witchcraft flattery, and it's not shrinking back. It's adding what you're called to do to what they already did. This reformation will expose areas where many were chasing their own glory and will frustrate all institutionalized assignments that are not kingdom assignments.

Jesus was the original pioneer of *all* pioneers. It's time to shake off the fear of man and walk on the path He already carved for every pioneer who would follow after Him. To be more concerned with the kingdom than recognition. It's a kingdom that has no end. The heart of the Father is partnership. The heart of the crowd is fickle especially when you start preaching a message that exposes error in the church. Even Jesus said so:

> "Anyone who comes to me must be willing to share my cross and experience it as his own, or he cannot

be considered to be my disciple. So don't follow me without considering what it will cost you. For who would construct a house before first sitting down to estimate the cost to complete it? Otherwise he may lay the foundation and not be able to finish. The neighbors will ridicule him, saying, 'Look at him! He started to build but couldn't complete it!'"
—Luke 14:27-30 (TPT)

If you have ever experienced that kind of resistance when you gently nudge against a wall that isn't ready to come down but NEEDS to come down, *you may be a pioneer in a reformation.* God has used man's disapproval and rejection over and over and over again in my life to crush the fear of man out of me. Following Jesus will cost you everything. I have been like Elijah, seeing powerful moves of God in one season and chased into caves of isolation by Jezebel chatter trying to shut down my calling the very next. You will have your own giants to face.

I'm just sharing from my limited experience and perspective, but what I have observed is that when a territorial spirit can no longer hold territory, control, manipulate, or intimidate you into submission and silence, it will often morph into much more insidious forms of control like rejection, spiritualized abuse, or accusation masquerading as discernment to prevent you from pioneering any further into its territory. You take this giant down with an identity rooted in the love of the Father and by not bowing down to its threats. You war with the promises of God, and you take that ground He has called you to occupy.

**YOU WAR WITH THE PROMISES OF
GOD, AND YOU TAKE THAT GROUND
HE HAS CALLED YOU TO OCCUPY.**

His response to Elijah was the same response to me and the same response to you: "Get out of your cave of isolation and go back the same way you came." Keep pastoring. Keep writing. Keep worshiping. Keep loving people. Keep pioneering. Keep mothering. Keep fathering. Keep birthing moves. Keep prophesying. Keep preaching. Keep serving. Keep resting. Keep healing. Keep being. Keep declaring the word of the Lord, and just do it. Do it rejected. Do it wounded. Do it with arrows sticking out of your back. DO IT.

Pioneers, you will reach a tipping point if you haven't already, where you will have to decide who called you. There are days you're going to struggle to even get out of bed. I've been there. The enemy could quickly turn very real offense into bitterness if we are not careful to continually love, forgive, release, and bless what can't be reconciled. Character assassination can be so insidious and ridiculous to the point you feel like something sacred died in you.

One day after school, when I was a little girl, the bus dropped me off at the end of the long dirt road to my house. I'd walked that dirt road many times. This day was different because I noticed a big bull had gotten out of the pen, and there was nothing separating me from him. He could have easily killed me. I didn't have any place to run and hide, so I started praying and running for my life as fast as my short little legs would take me to the safety of the cattle guard that prevented the bull from following me the rest of the way home.

If you've ever experienced retaliation from a Jezebel spirit, then you know it's a lot like *that*. It's an angry bull using intimidation and threatening advances that make us feel isolated from safety. Our battle isn't with people. It's a spirit trying to stop you from moving freely in God's purposes, and if it has stopped you, it's definitely time to *return*. There is a cattle guard for your soul. A place of safety and covering where you can run and hide, and the enemy has no access.

SAFETY FOR YOUR SOUL LOOKS LIKE:
» Going back to family.
» Going back to presence.
» Going back to Scripture.
» Going back to your assignment.
» Going back to the wild.

It's the Lord saying to you what He said to Elijah: "Go back the same way you came, and travel to the wilderness of Damascus" (1 Kings 19:15, NLT). "Go back to the wilderness I called you to before the enemy hijacked what I was about to birth through you there. Go back. I will fight for you and vindicate this season if you hold your peace, be still, and go back to doing what I called you to do." When He sends you back the same way you came, you don't walk the same. You don't talk the same. You don't think the same. You don't worship the same.

The road is the same, the situation is the same, but you're not the same. He's doing something new in YOU.

The path where you feared for your life is now the place where you find your family. The path where you lost your voice is now the place you will use it. The path where you were rejected is the place you walk in your next assignment. Your pain will not be wasted. Everything that was lost, heaven will return, and the Lord will provide:

> So Elijah went and found Elisha son of Shaphat plowing a field. There were twelve teams of oxen in the field, and Elisha was plowing with the twelfth team. Elijah went over to him and threw his cloak across his shoulders and then walked away.
> —1 Kings 19:19 (NLT)

Eventually, every tree reveals itself by the fruit, and every scheme of hell gets exposed for what it really is too. The magnitude of restitution you're about to receive for how you stayed low and honoring in your season of shaking and sifting is going to be more than your arms can carry. Those who come behind you will be picking up treasure from your overflow. You will take the land. You will find your people. You will come out of this fire refined like gold. We have a Guardian God on our side. The original pioneering Good Shepherd of our soul, who goes before us and behind us and makes a way to safety. He gives us a sound mind in place of the spirit of fear. He lifts us out of the fog of confusion.

Let the Lord be your defender. Exodus 14:14 promises that the Lord will fight for you. Just be still. Stay calm. Hold your peace. He is about to overwhelm everything that tried to overwhelm you. Don't get sucked into trying to clear your name. Stay pure. The fruit will do that for you. Every place you were rejected will be a place where you experience promotion IF you keep your heart right.

It's important to know that if you're walking through a similar season, the justice system of heaven looks like a cross. The Lord doesn't ever treat us as our sin deserves, and He doesn't treat our enemies the way their sin deserves. We're all growing in the fullness of Christlike maturity. He is kind and gracious and merciful to ALL who turn to Him. I need that mercy every day too. Our battle isn't against people but principalities. The enemy will use people who partner with him to carry out his plans, but Satan is always the one behind the curtain pulling the strings. Don't speak against people out of your wound. That's vengeance. It belongs to God. You know your heart is getting right when you can sincerely want the best for people who wanted the worst for you.

HIS VENGEANCE ISN'T SMITING OUR ACCUSERS. IT'S GIVING US A MINISTRY IN THE VERY AREA WE WERE ONCE A VICTIM.

Get healed and let your wound become a testimony His glory can rest on. That is how God gets revenge against the enemy. His vengeance isn't smiting our accusers. It's giving us a ministry in the very area we were once a victim. The anointing and word resting on your life will also be your test, and your test will be the greenhouse for every good promise of the Lord. God deeply loves the people who deeply wound us. Forgive. Release them. Cut the strings of offense and give them back to Jesus. Give Him your ashes too. Jesus is a better judge. Jesus knows how to make beauty from ashes. Leave it with Him because like He did for Joseph, He's working it out for your good: "As for you, you meant evil against me, but God meant it for good, to bring it about that many people should be kept alive, as they are today" (Genesis 50:20, ESV).

I walked through one particularly painful pioneering season when a father in my life called me on the phone and spoke to me as a daughter. With a father's authority, he said, "Rhea, you are not to receive these arrows of accusation. They did not come from the Lord. They are attempts to shut down your calling. Don't let them."

I'll never forget that when he said that, I let out this deep, undignified cry of deliverance, and healing flowed out on holy ground like someone pulled the release valve that had been blocking an ocean of grief in my soul. The discouragement and oppression of that season lifted so fast when a father spoke truth over my identity.

Fathers and mothers are the OG pioneers. You do not know the power of your voice and the authority on your mantle to lead sons and daughters through kingdom reformation! Before seeking to be good at anything, seek to be a good father and a good mother. Paul says we have ten thousand babysitters but not many fathers. Fathers and mothers have a governmental anointing. This isn't about age. It's about willingness to bring the truthful and loving voice of God to situations. So before the enemy can mess with sons and daughters, he has to go through fathers and mothers to get to them. Our words build worlds and form destinies. Maybe the title we should really be craving in our churches is "Mom" or "Dad."

God can use very real rejection to set you free from a spirit of rejection and the fear of man. Maybe He wouldn't let you leave because there was very real deliverance in the very fire that tried to consume you. And let me tell you, getting out from underneath that oppression is like the first breath of air after the waves have pounded you into the rocks. God will not waste your pain! He is turning it into costly oil.

Jesus was crushed in the olive press wearing OUR judgment, so we could be filled with the oil of His sacrifice. He yielded His life to the crushing while some friends slept and others conspired for selfish gain. Lips that kissed him with brotherly affection were the same lips that issued a kiss of betrayal. Our hearts get just as twisted when we spend our lives with divided affections. No amount of ministry can make up for our lack of love for Him. We have to keep our focus pure because we all have capacity to be a Judas.

If you have ever experienced anything remotely like this, I'm so sorry. Let me encourage you with this truth I discovered while running for my life into my own cave of isolation. Pioneers value purity over popularity. Period. Pioneering is hard, painful, misunderstood work that comes with pushback and crushing and even suffering—but also beauty and legacy and fruitfulness because our reward is Jesus.

I feel like training grounds sometimes do a disservice to those called into full-time vocational ministry. We really hype up our classrooms and altar calls without warning anybody what it actually costs to follow Jesus. So let me help you now. It will cost you everything:

> You will be hated by all because of my life in you. But don't worry. My grace will never desert you or depart from your life. Stand firm with patient endurance and you will find your soul's deliverance.
> —Luke 21:17-19 (TPT)

But Jesus is worth everything: "I am convinced that any suffering we endure is less than nothing compared to the magnitude of glory that is about to be unveiled within us" (Romans 8:18, TPT).

YOU + JESUS − FAMILY = A CULT WAITING TO HAPPEN.

Jesus was always clear about the cost and the risk. He didn't want anyone to be surprised. Yet, somehow, we still are. Pioneers don't turn back when things get hard. Pioneers showed up expecting cuts and bruises and danger in the first place. They let the Holy Spirit tend to their wounds. What they don't do is stop. They don't always know where they're going next; all they know is they can't stay where they've been. If you do it right, people may never know your name or what you did, but they will be in awe at how much easier their journey was because a pioneer traveled ahead of them.

A lot of pioneers have stood alone because nobody else was going that way at the time. However, there are also those who CHOOSE to go alone, and that is a slippery slope because God hardwired us for family.

You + Jesus−Family = A cult waiting to happen.

Pioneers are human and, therefore, not immune to the attacks of the enemy.

10 ROADBLOCKS TO PIONEERING:
1) Distractions.
2) Divided affections.
3) Old manna.
4) Building things Jesus didn't ask for.
5) Going places He didn't send you.
6) Unrepentant sin.
7) Seeking the top instead of the bottom.
8) Fighting battles you weren't called to.
9) Striving.
10) Offense and isolation.

Being a pioneer is an invitation to personal reformation. It's an invitation to being misunderstood. It's an invitation to the backside of a wilderness. That wilderness isn't punishment. It's the place of preparation and purification. The place where you root your identity deeply in the Father's affection and not in titles and assignments. The place where you die to your flesh. The place where you die to the compulsion to be relevant and important. The place where you shake off the fear of man and finally DO the thing Christ has called you to do. Pioneers are birthed in the struggle. They are the Isaiahs saying, "Here am I. Send me." Giving their yes before He even asks.

You will discover how much it costs to obey. You'll have to contend for what the Lord has spoken over your life, and you'll have to contend for the land He has called you to when nobody else BUT God believes in it. Don't quit when it costs more than you bargained for. Maturity isn't fast *or* cheap. Discipleship is not easy, which is why so many churches settle for performers. The rejection a pioneer faces is actually birthing. He can't do big things through you until He does deep things in you. Will you keep touching His heart when nobody understands? Pouring your oil on HIM when it's not received by people? Obeying when you lose your crowd? Keeping your worship pure when it's not popular? We sacrifice way too many things God values on the altar of relevance.

When you're dead to the point that you question everything you always thought you were, that's a seed that holds unfathomable potential. Your test will be your greenhouse, and God will reward a pioneer's progress with painful pruning that doesn't feel like a reward. Hold on, though. Your costly little seed is about to grow into a wild jungle. Value doesn't come from others affirming your value. Value came from Jesus. Whether others affirm it or not, it's settled in heaven; now let it be settled in you. He will not leave this work in you unfinished.

My first word was "horse." I've always felt at home around them. Either on the back of one swimming down a river or spending hours having "conversations" with them as a child snuggled nose to nose. I had a dream one night that I was running at the front of a band of wild horses that were so fast, and somehow, I was keeping up effortlessly and having the time of my life. It reminded me of God's rebuke to Jeremiah: "If racing against mere men makes you tired, how will you race against horses? If you stumble and fall on open ground, what will you do in the thickets near the Jordan?" (Jeremiah 12:5, NLT). And it feels like a word for the church in this hour. Jeremiah was confused with the Lord's justice. It felt as though God was allowing the wicked to prosper. He had known the God who answered all his prayers with yes. Now he was learning about His lordship. Ever been there?

He was learning about the God with sovereign authority to move against the will of man in ways too high for our understanding. How to stay planted in obedience when it doesn't work out the way you immediately assume it should. Staying faithful when God doesn't move how we expect him to is a test every pioneer has faced or will face. Jeremiah was asking an appropriate question in an honoring way. He was worn out by those who loved God with their lips but not with their actions. Can you relate? Worn out by religion? Worn out by compromise? Worn out by wickedness that seems to thrive unchecked? Attacked for doing what's right? Jeremiah said the wickedness was so bad animals and plants were dying because the land was physically groaning.

God's response to Jeremiah was basically this:

> "Jeremiah, there will be a coming season of compassion, and my goal is redemption, but first I need to

crush the pride and rebellion out of my people, so I will give them over to their wicked, carnal desires, so they can see their need for me. So buckle up. Harder battles are coming. If this wears you out how, will you handle what's next? If you get discouraged when you can openly see the wickedness, how will you handle the season of HIDDEN subterfuge trying to take you out? Like navigating the flood plains of the Jordan with its wild jungle overgrowth and hidden snares and lions prowling to devour you?"

God was basically saying, "If the battle you see trips you up, how will you walk steadily in harder battles you CAN'T see? Let me teach you to suffer well and endure and grow." Pioneers know how to suffer well without blaming or retaliating. In Psalm 73:13-14 (author paraphrase), we see David ask a similar question: "Am I keeping my life pure for nothing? I'm following all the rules, and people with wicked agendas are still prospering." And God showed David the answer to the same frustration Jeremiah was having. All who sin against God are on a slippery slope to judgment, and God is a God of justice, never falling asleep on that job one time since the dawn of time.

ALL WHO SIN AGAINST GOD ARE ON A SLIPPERY SLOPE TO JUDGMENT, AND GOD IS A GOD OF JUSTICE, NEVER FALLING ASLEEP ON THAT JOB ONE TIME SINCE THE DAWN OF TIME.

What was David's response? In Psalm 73:26 (NLT), he said, "My health may fail, and my spirit may grow weak, but God remains the strength of my heart; he is mine forever." David learned how to run with horses. This is how we run with horses and how we go the distance. When you're abused and others prosper. When things don't go the way you prayed. When doors close in your face. When people you love betray you. When you're faithful and still suffer. When you are dishonored by people you've sacrificed so much for. When cycles don't break and heartbreak returns. When people misrepresent your heart. By desiring Jesus more than any other thing on earth, in the middle of the suffering, you will learn to run with the horses.

God is not slow in keeping His promises. He is outside of time. God is building our endurance for harder battles coming. It's not always going to be so safe and comfortable, church. The western church has grown so sleepy and Jesus is still looking for friends who will stay awake with Him. We have to graduate from knowing Jesus as Savior to fearing Him as Lord. He is good even when things are not good. Our circumstances don't reflect His nature. He is more than our Deliverer. He is what we're being delivered *to*!

The prize was always Him, pioneer. So suffer well, and don't allow your love to wax cold. Joy is not a feeling. It's a Person named Jesus, and you can have as much of Him as you want. Don't settle for crumbs when Jesus invites you to feast on the whole meal of who He is. The revival on the inside eventually has to move out. If it stays in you, it will die in you. It's a wild flowing river leading to a promised land. Every promised land comes with opportunity and opposition. There is a reward when the giants fall! Our faith increases. Our stewardship gets better. The report we believe to be true about the Lord, will always be the report we spread. We can be like Caleb in Numbers 13:30 (NLT): "Let's go at once to take the land.... We can certainly conquer it!"

God didn't say we should be comfortable and stand still. He said to be FRUITFUL and MULTIPLY. Don't allow the warfare and retaliation of the enemy to keep you out of your promised land. Don't allow what you see in the natural to talk you out of the supernatural help God is sending you. You have wild new frontiers to conquer and subdue. The enemy is getting louder because you're getting closer. He will do everything in his power to make the blueprints in your hand feel like a grasshopper in a land of giants. But that tiny blueprint is a dream in the heart of the Father and holds the power of the ages.

Kingdom pioneers, let God break every ladder of striving in your life. Don't lose your fire. Don't allow your love to grow cold, your heart to grow calloused, or your purity to be diluted by mixture. Don't sacrifice your family on the altar of performance-building Jesus never asked for. Your value isn't in assignments or the esteem of men. It's hidden in Christ. Accusations can't diminish it, and rejection can't cancel it. You're overcoming stagnation and apathy. Not one single weapon formed to keep you out of your assignment has prospered.

You're moving forward to a wild frontier with unimaginable possibilities. It's a new day. Obedience is your only job now. You're retiring formulas and stepping into the flowing river of God. This ends in a wedding. Go low. Protect your oil. Stay wild. Be free from rejection and the fear of man. Be led by the Spirit and aligned to His Word. Keep your love pure and your heart free from offense. Only build what Jesus asks for—and build it *with* Him. You're not stuck. It's not over. It's just getting started. So, be a pioneer like the first disciples: "Immediately, they dropped their nets and left everything behind to follow Jesus." (Matthew 4:20, TPT).

> **PIONEER PRAYER:**
> *God, I receive Your commissioning to a wild, unshakable kingdom and a life of personal revival. What the world calls balance, you call mixture, and I will not be double-minded about following You. I will shake off the dust of past rejection and embrace the new wineskin you have for me, however costly it may be. I will go first and be the bottom of whatever you want to build on my laid-down life so that others can go higher. The road is paved with difficulties, but I will forge new paths, birth the dreams of Your heart, and finish my race. In Jesus's name. Amen.*

Pioneer Prompt:

You are stepping out of the wilderness, healed and whole. In your hand is a map. You can't go back, and you can't stay where you've been. It's time to move, unlock the move you've been birthing in secret, and release it on the earth for the glory of God. Where does the map lead next? What do you need to drop and leave behind to fully follow Jesus? Journal what God shows you.

_____

_____

_____

_____

_____

_____

_____

_____

_____

_____

_____

_____

www.ingramcontent.com/pod-product-compliance
Lightning Source LLC
Chambersburg PA
CBHW050854160426
43194CB00011B/2153